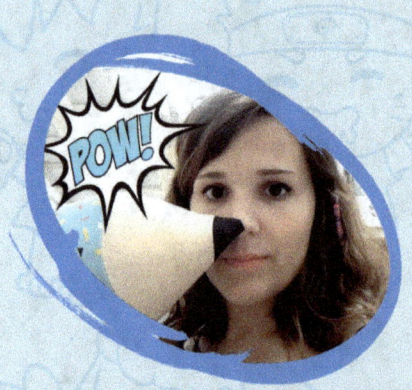

"AS A PROFESSIONAL ILLUSTRATOR WITH A DEGREE IN EARLY
CHILDHOOD EDUCATION, I HAVE WANTED TO CREATE THIS BOOK TO
COMBINE MY TWO PASSIONS: TEACHING AND DRAWING. THANKS TO
THOSE WONDERFUL MOMENTS I'VE ENJOYED DRAWING WITH MY
FAMILY, TEACHING CHILDREN HOW TO DRAW, AND SEEING THEM
ENJOY COLORING MY ILLUSTRATIONS, I'VE BEEN INSPIRED TO
CREATE THESE PAGES.
I DEDICATE THIS BOOK TO MY GODDAUGHTER WITH ALL THE LOVE
IN THE WORLD SO THAT SHE WILL ALWAYS REMEMBER THE GOOD
TIMES FILLED WITH CREATIVITY THAT SHE HAS ENJOYED WITH HER
GODMOTHER.

· FOR CAROLINA.

INDEX

WHAT IS KAWAII?

THE WORD 'KAWAII' COMES FROM JAPANESE, AND ITS MEANING IS SIMILAR TO 'BLUSH.' HOWEVER, TODAY WE REFER TO ANYTHING 'KAWAII' AS SOMETHING 'ADORABLE OR CUTE'.

THE KAWAII STYLE IS ADOPTED BY MANY ARTISTS WORLDWIDE. IT IS CHARACTERIZED BY THE USE OF ROUNDED, SIMPLIFIED SHAPES, NO NOSES, AND LARGE EYES. IT CAN BE APPLIED TO CHARACTERS, ANIMALS, EVERYDAY OBJECTS, AND EVEN FOOD. SOME ARTISTS EVEN INCORPORATE IT DIRECTLY INTO PHOTOGRAPHY.

NOT ALL ARTISTS FOLLOW THE SAME RULES WHEN USING THE KAWAII STYLE. YOU CAN FIND KAWAII CHARACTERS WITHOUT MOUTHS, WITH SMALLER EYES, AND EVEN THOUGH THEY USUALLY HAVE FEW DETAILS, SOME ARTISTS LIKE TO ADD DETAIL TO THE HANDS, HAIR, OR CLOTHING OF THEIR CREATIONS.

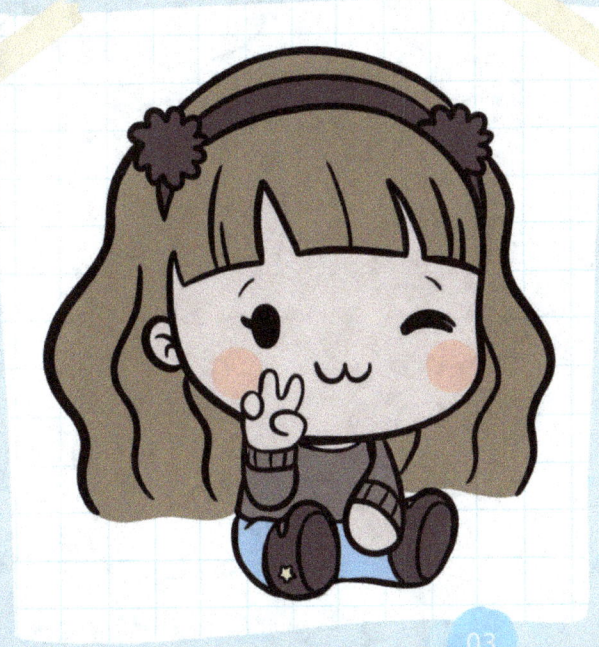

I'M GOING TO TEACH YOU THE BASIC CONCEPTS FOR CREATING YOUR CHARACTERS. I'LL SHOW YOU HOW TO MAKE KAWAII PEOPLE AND ANIMALS, AS WELL AS HOW TO BRING FUN AND ADORABLE FOOD TO LIFE. WE'RE GOING TO HAVE A GREAT TIME DRAWING TOGETHER.

EXPRESSIONS

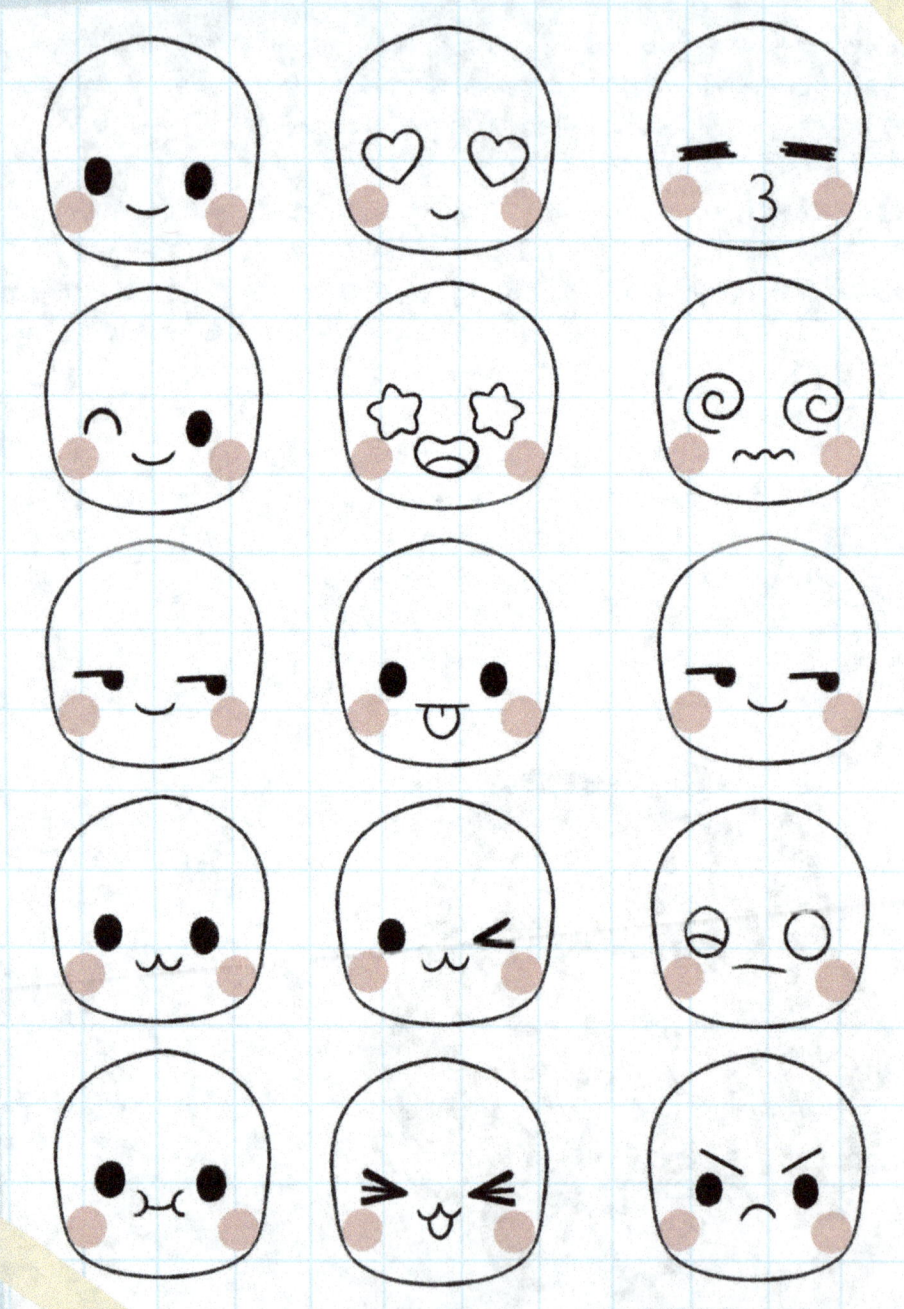

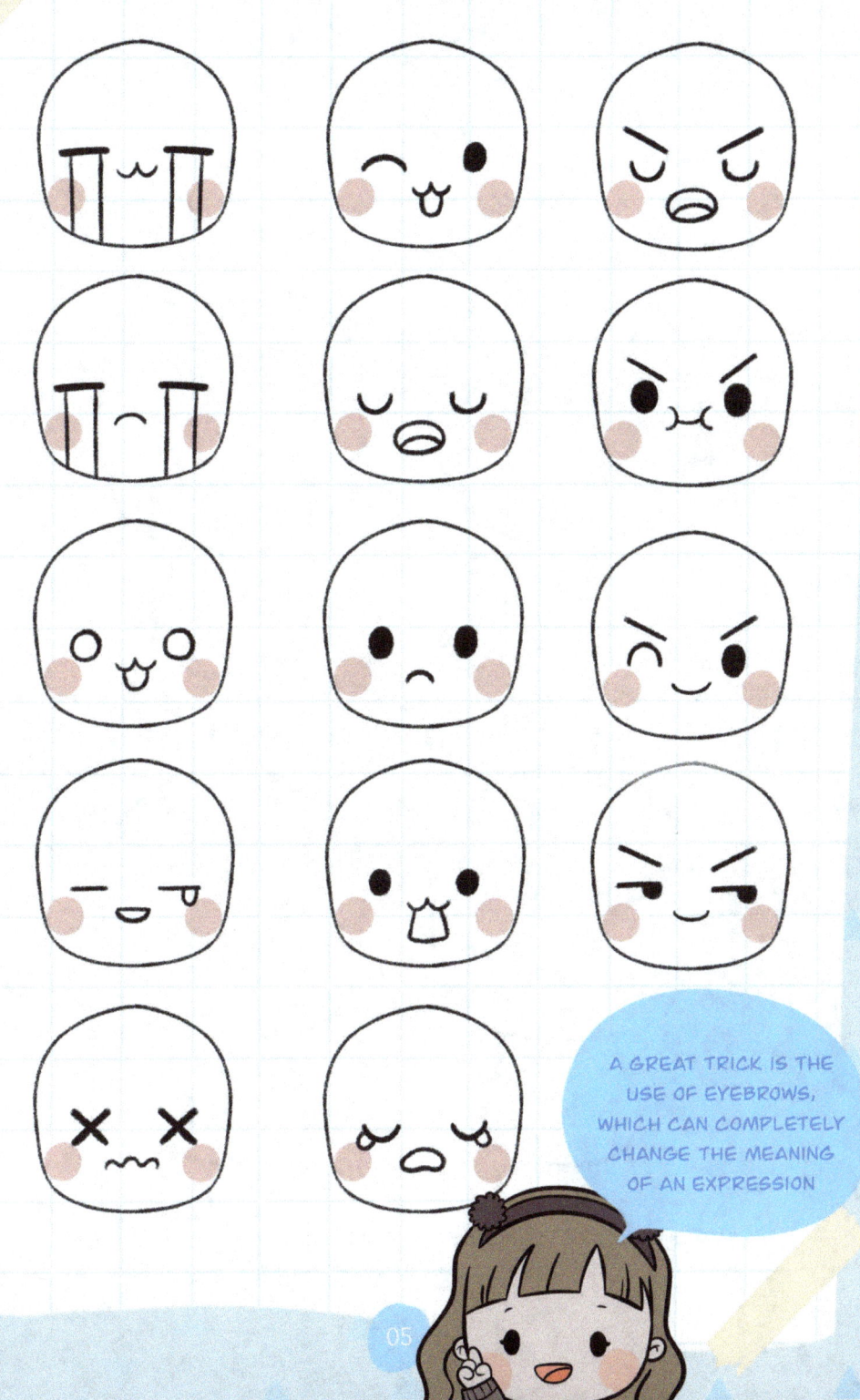

A GREAT TRICK IS THE USE OF EYEBROWS, WHICH CAN COMPLETELY CHANGE THE MEANING OF AN EXPRESSION

THE BODY

TO CREATE THE BODY, START WITH TWO VERY SIMPLE SHAPES, A CIRCLE AND A RECTANGLE WITH ROUNDED CORNERS. OVER THIS SKETCH, GIVE THE FIGURE SOME CURVES; IT WILL LOOK NICER.

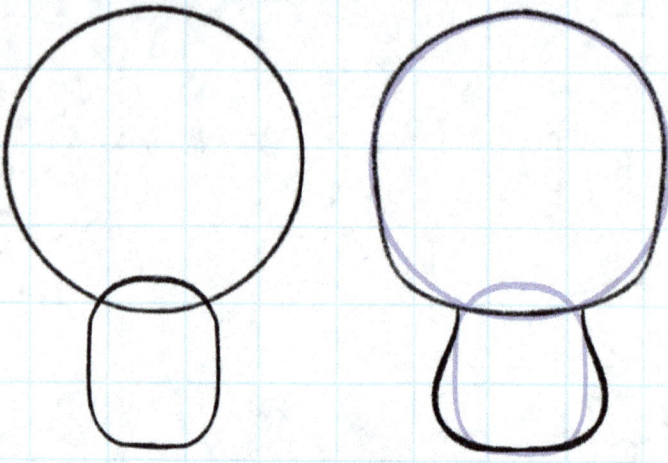

YOU HAVE TO PRACTICE THIS TECHNIQUE, AND IN THE END, IT WILL COME NATURALLY, WITHOUT NEEDING TO DRAW THE INITIAL SHAPES.

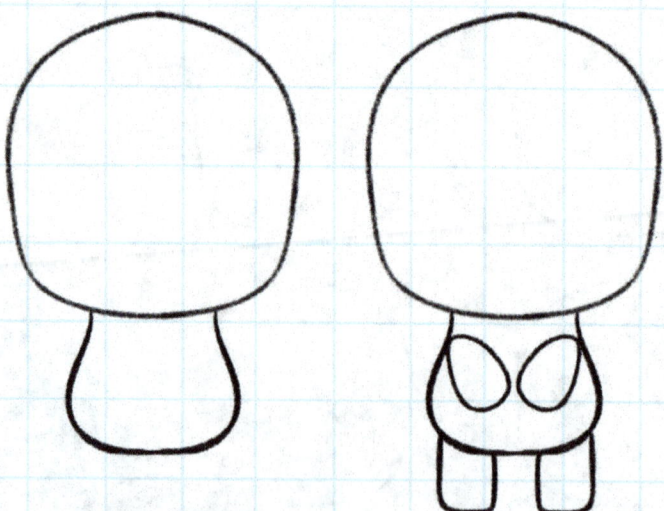

ADD SIMPLE LEGS AND ARMS IN THE SHAPE OF DROPS OR RECTANGLES WITH ROUNDED EDGES.

PROFILES

ALTHOUGH THE KAWAII STYLE IS CHARACTERIZED BY A SIMPLE FORWARD-FACING LOOK FOR THE CHARACTER, WE CAN ALSO PLAY WITH POSITIONS AND MOVEMENTS. HERE ARE SEVERAL PROFILES THAT CAN BE VERY USEFUL.

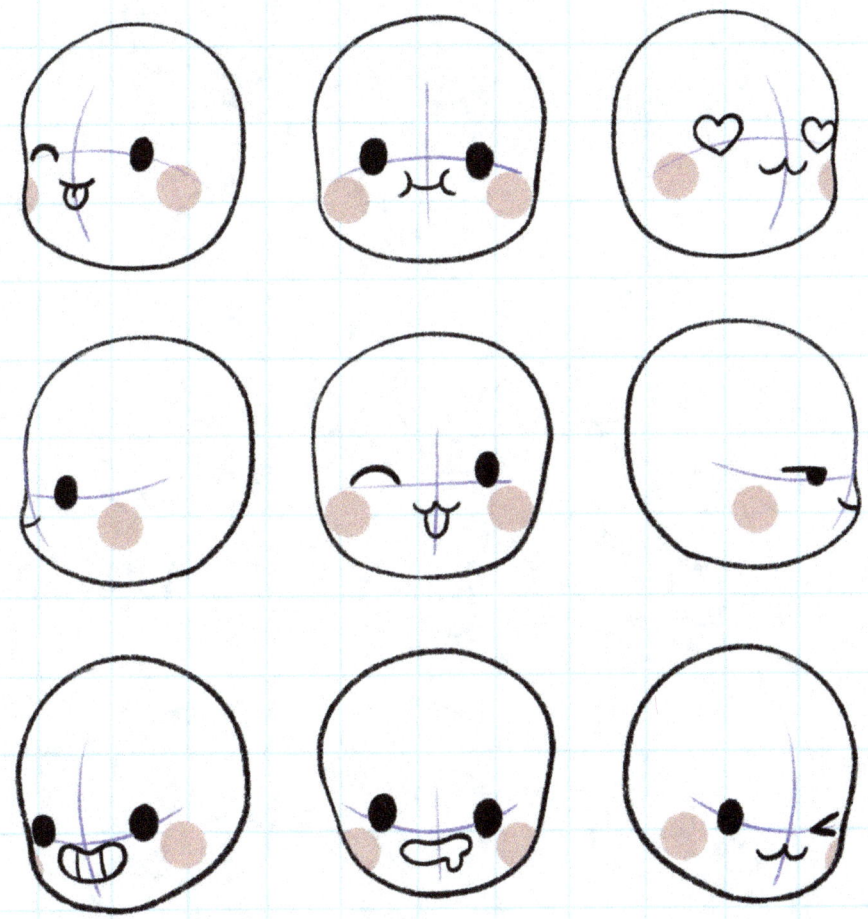

THE BLUE CROSS IS A FANTASTIC GUIDE TO HELP YOU PLACE THE EYES, NOSE, AND MOUTH CORRECTLY. NOW, TEST THE DIFFERENT PROFILES WITH VARIOUS EXPRESSIONS.

POSES

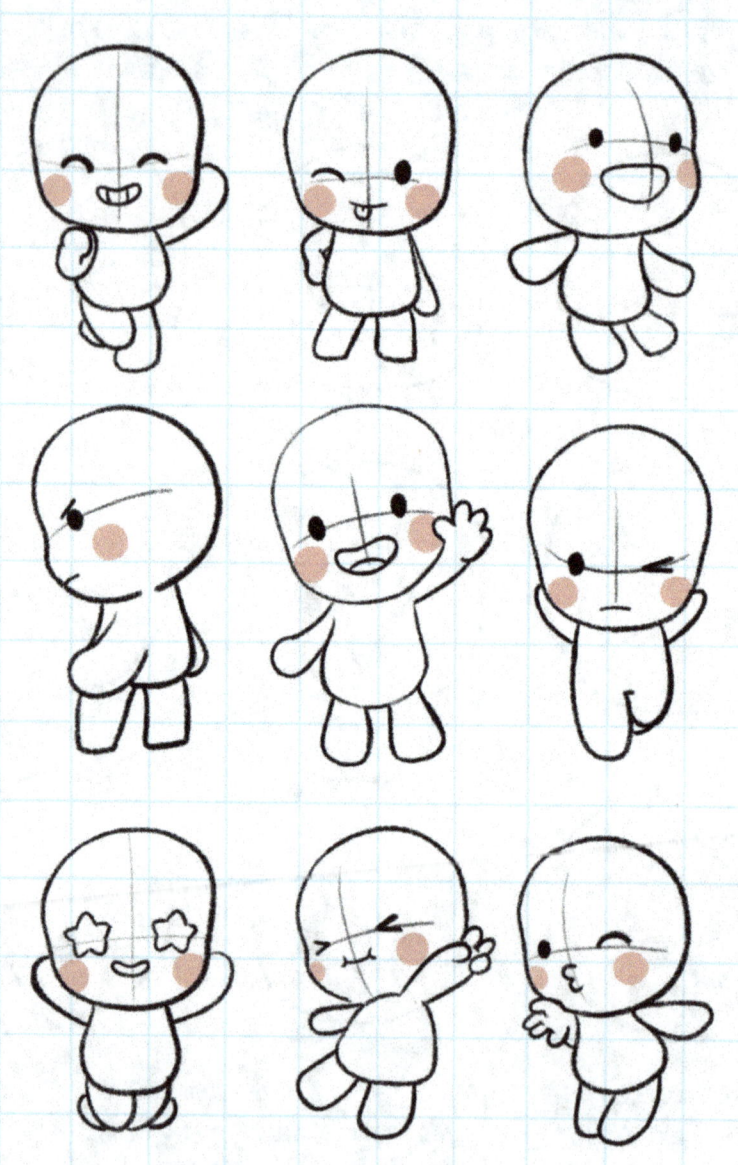

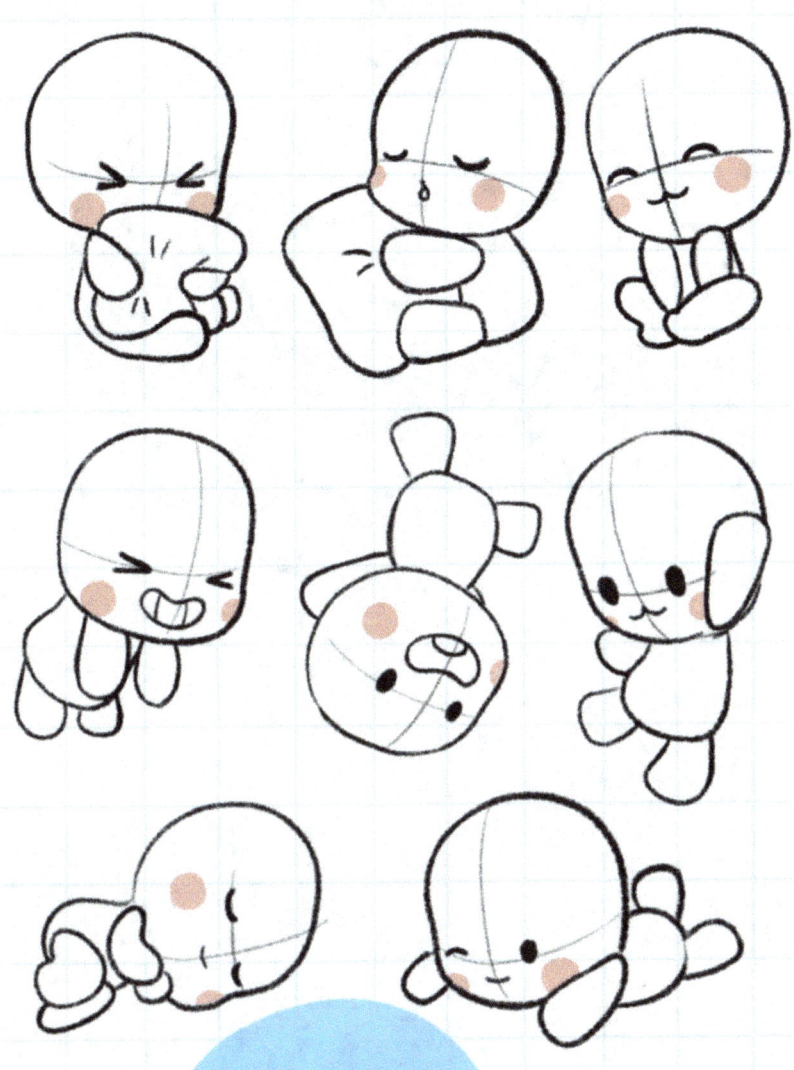

DON'T WORRY, NOW WE'RE GOING TO DRAW STEP BY STEP TOGETHER ALL THE POSES WITH SUPER CUTE AND FUN CHARACTERS.

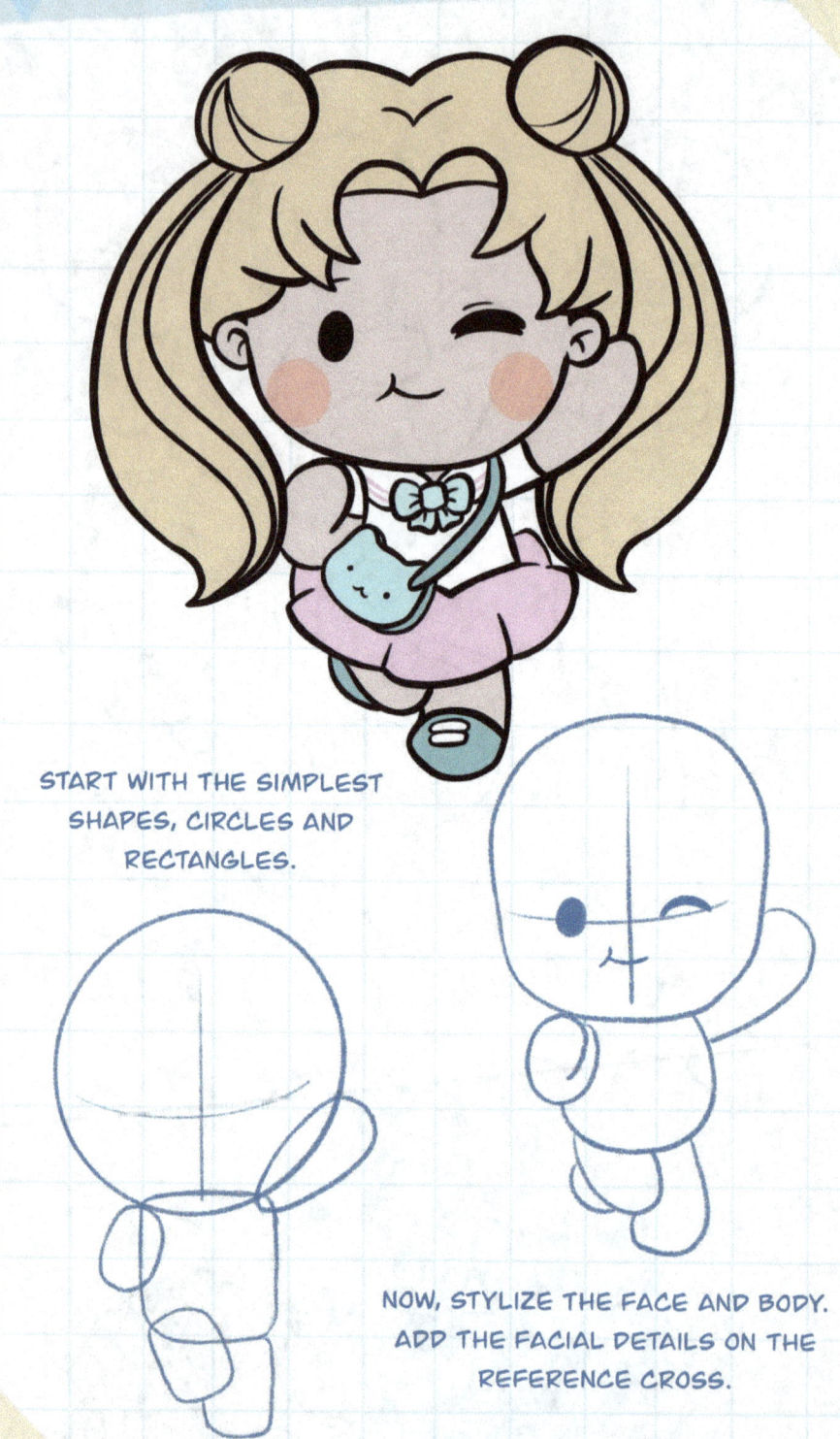

START WITH THE SIMPLEST
SHAPES, CIRCLES AND
RECTANGLES.

NOW, STYLIZE THE FACE AND BODY.
ADD THE FACIAL DETAILS ON THE
REFERENCE CROSS.

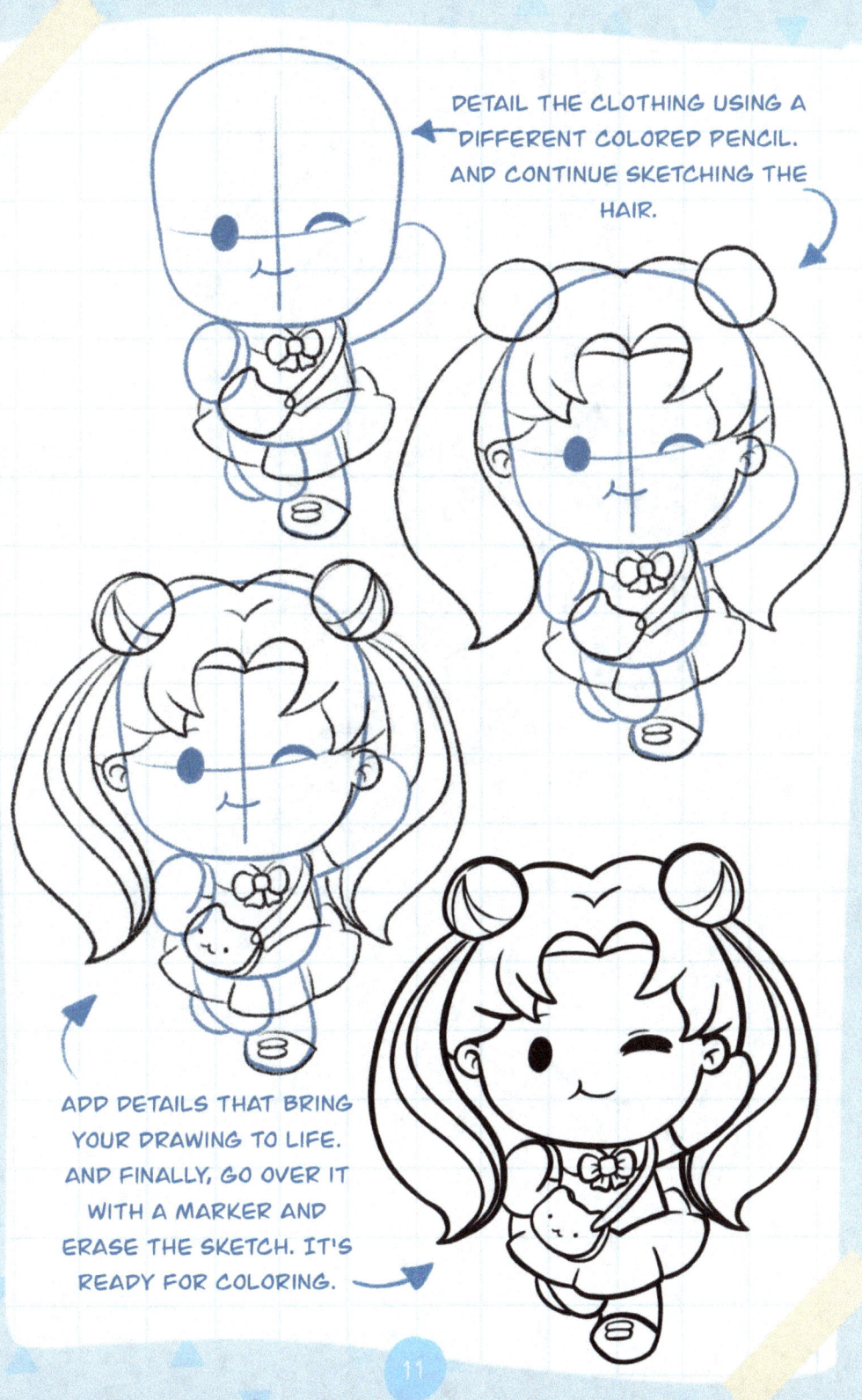

DETAIL THE CLOTHING USING A DIFFERENT COLORED PENCIL. AND CONTINUE SKETCHING THE HAIR.

ADD DETAILS THAT BRING YOUR DRAWING TO LIFE. AND FINALLY, GO OVER IT WITH A MARKER AND ERASE THE SKETCH. IT'S READY FOR COLORING.

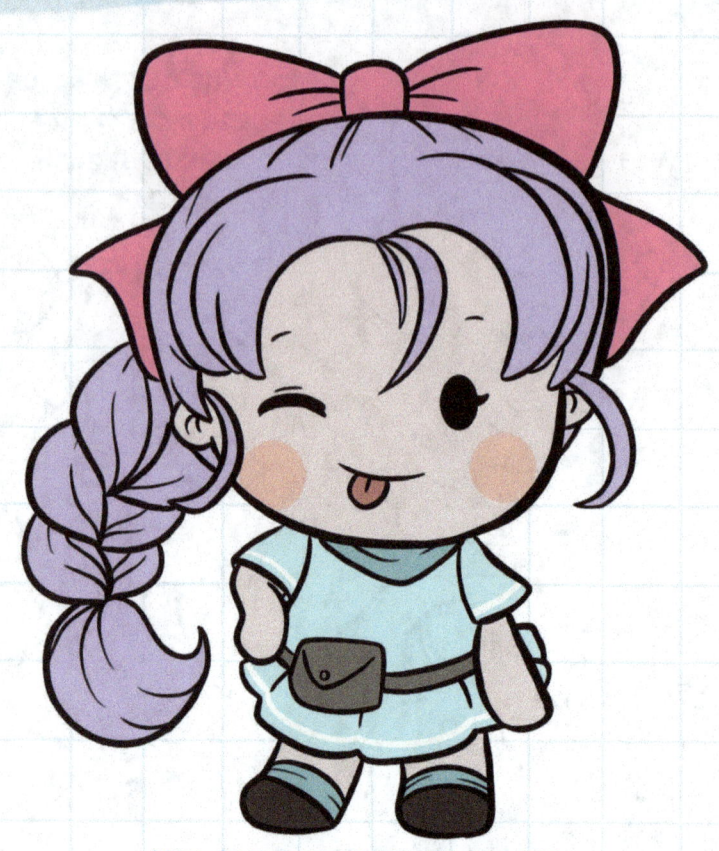

YOU CAN ADD FANTASY COLORS
TO YOUR CHARACTERS' HAIR.

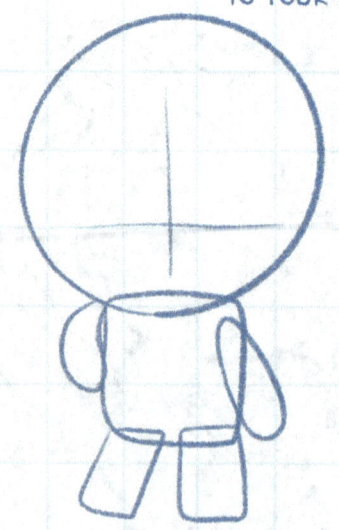

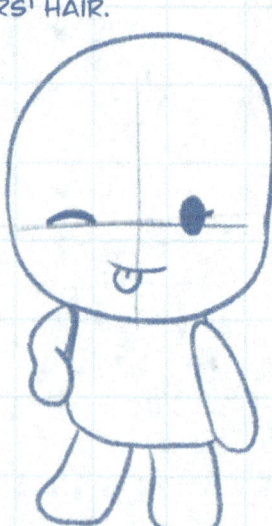

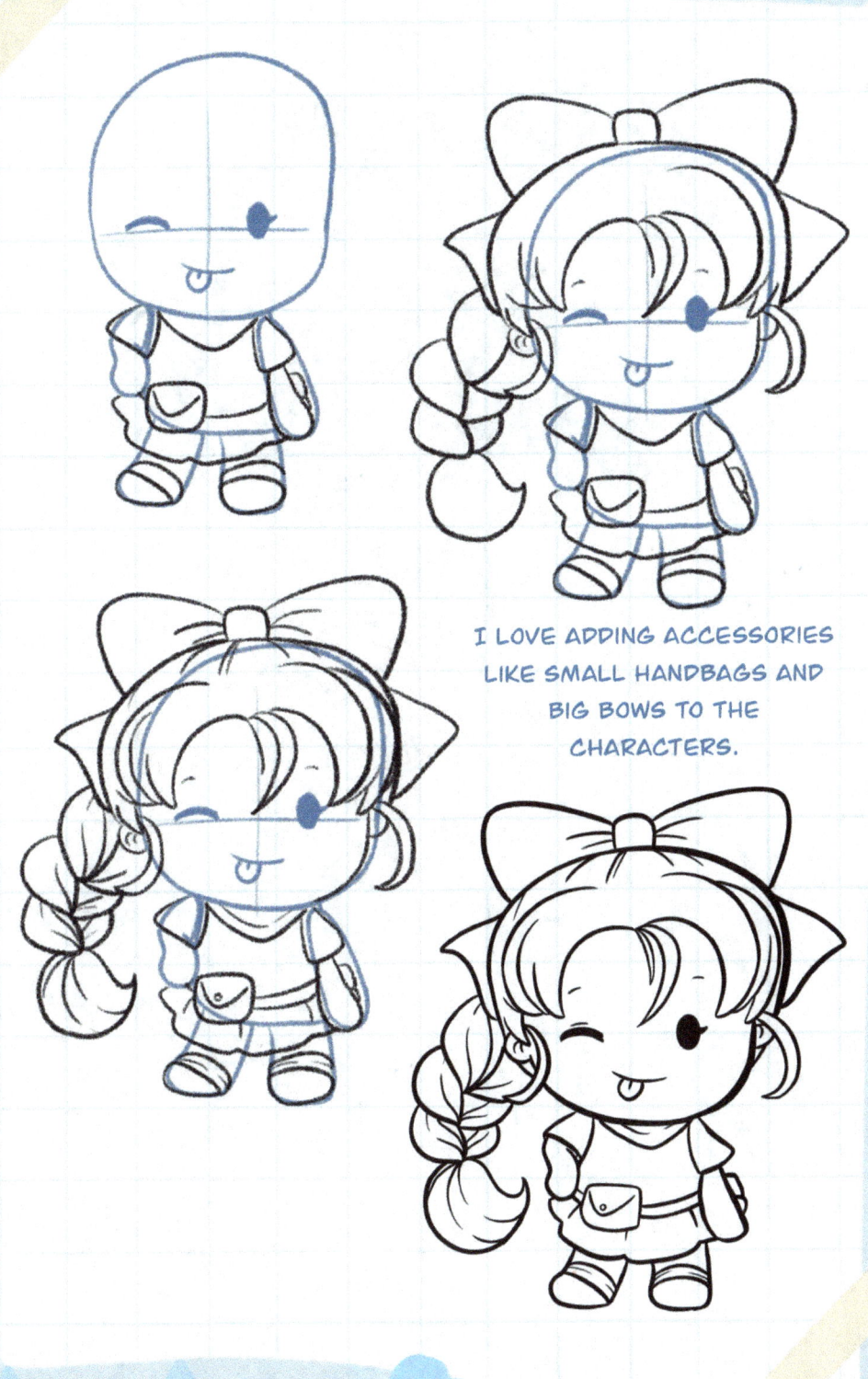

I LOVE ADDING ACCESSORIES LIKE SMALL HANDBAGS AND BIG BOWS TO THE CHARACTERS.

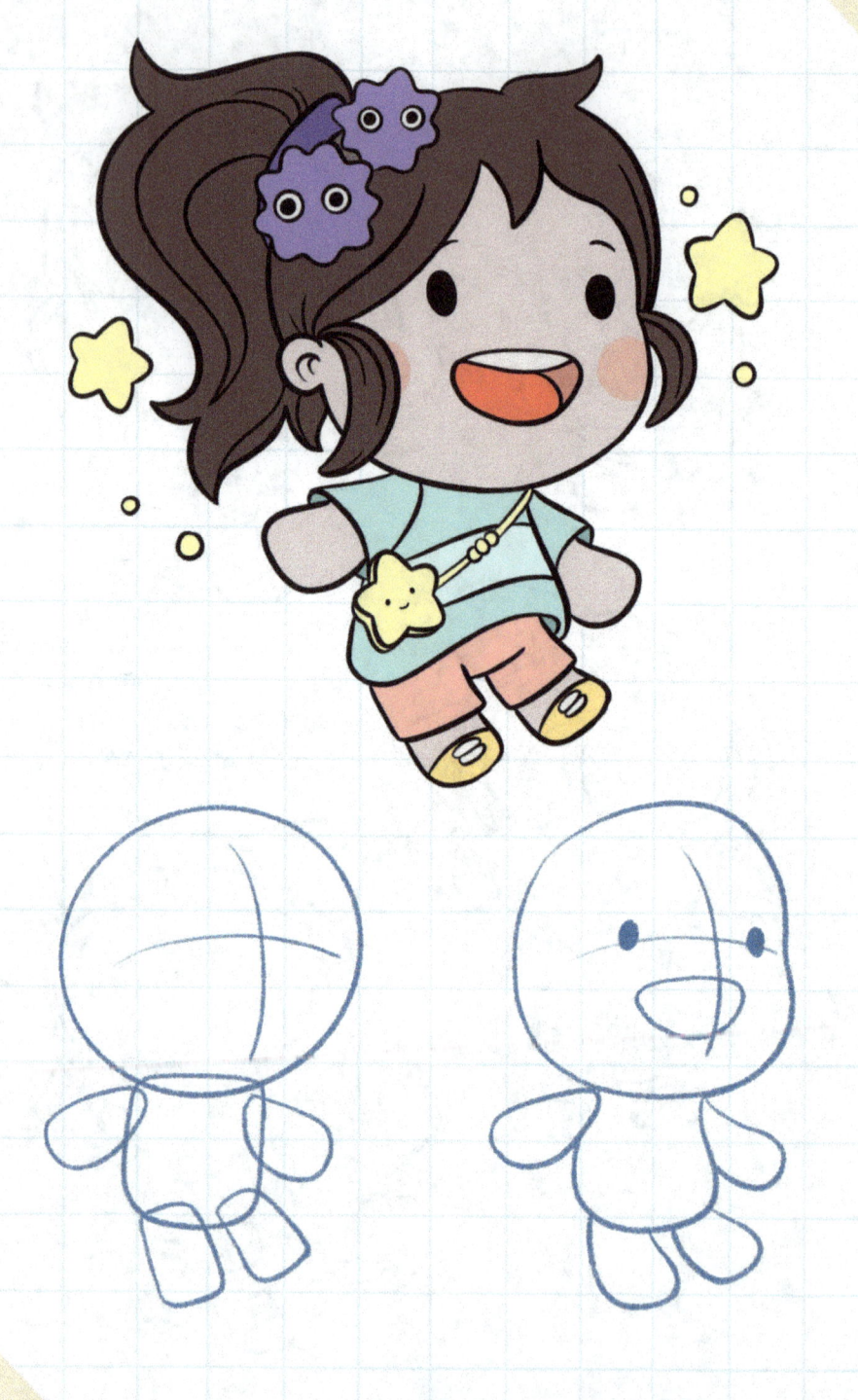

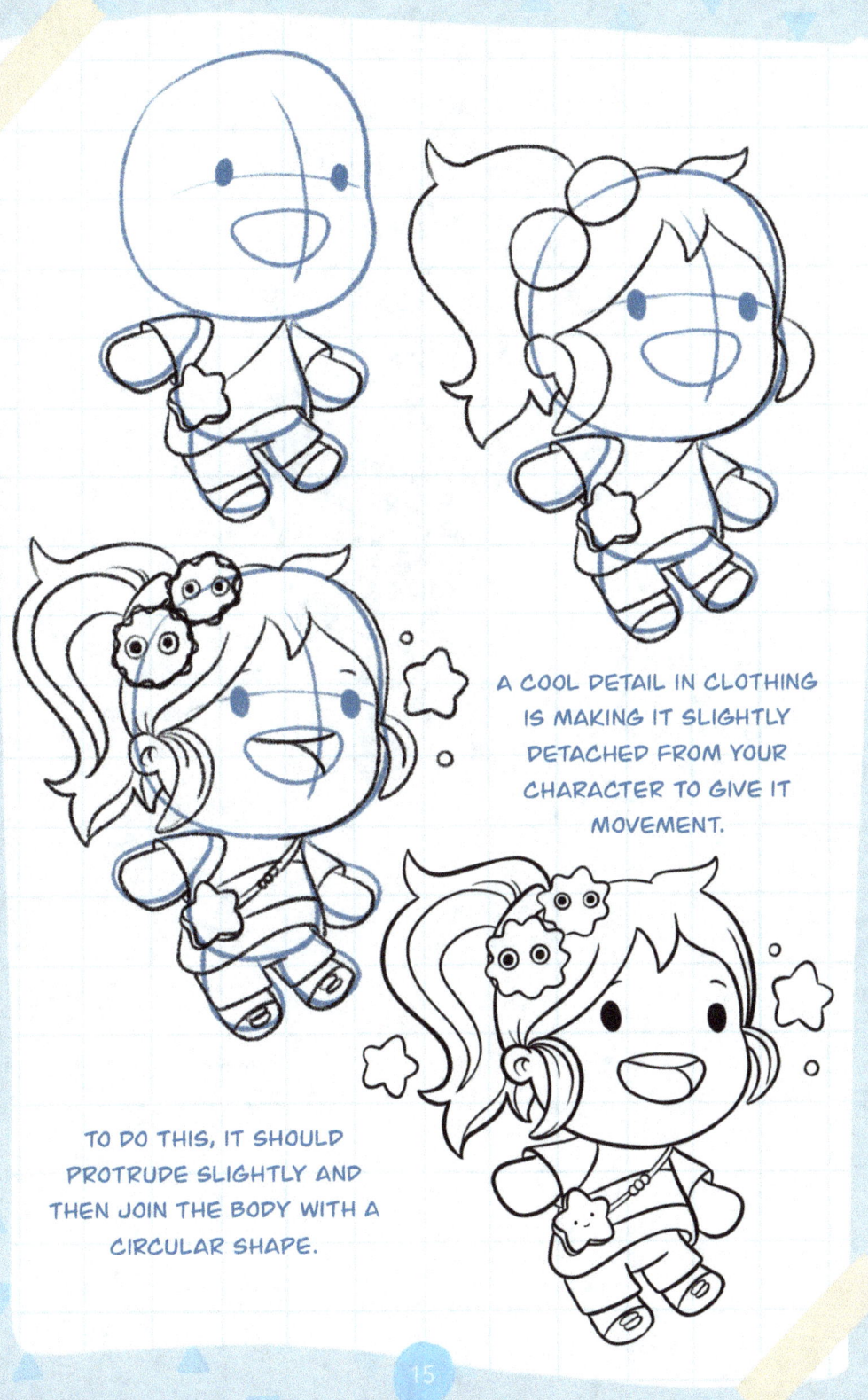

A COOL DETAIL IN CLOTHING IS MAKING IT SLIGHTLY DETACHED FROM YOUR CHARACTER TO GIVE IT MOVEMENT.

TO DO THIS, IT SHOULD PROTRUDE SLIGHTLY AND THEN JOIN THE BODY WITH A CIRCULAR SHAPE.

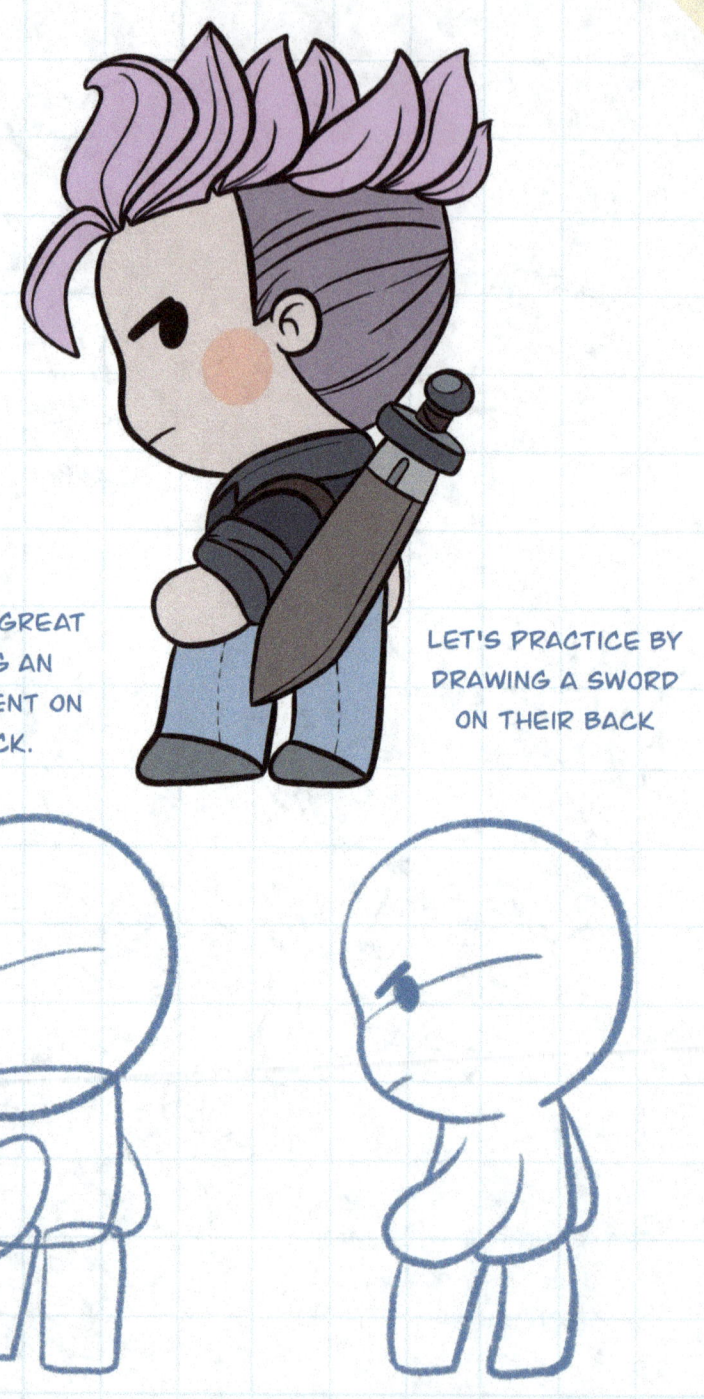

THIS POSE IS GREAT FOR ADDING AN EXTRA ELEMENT ON THEIR BACK.

LET'S PRACTICE BY DRAWING A SWORD ON THEIR BACK

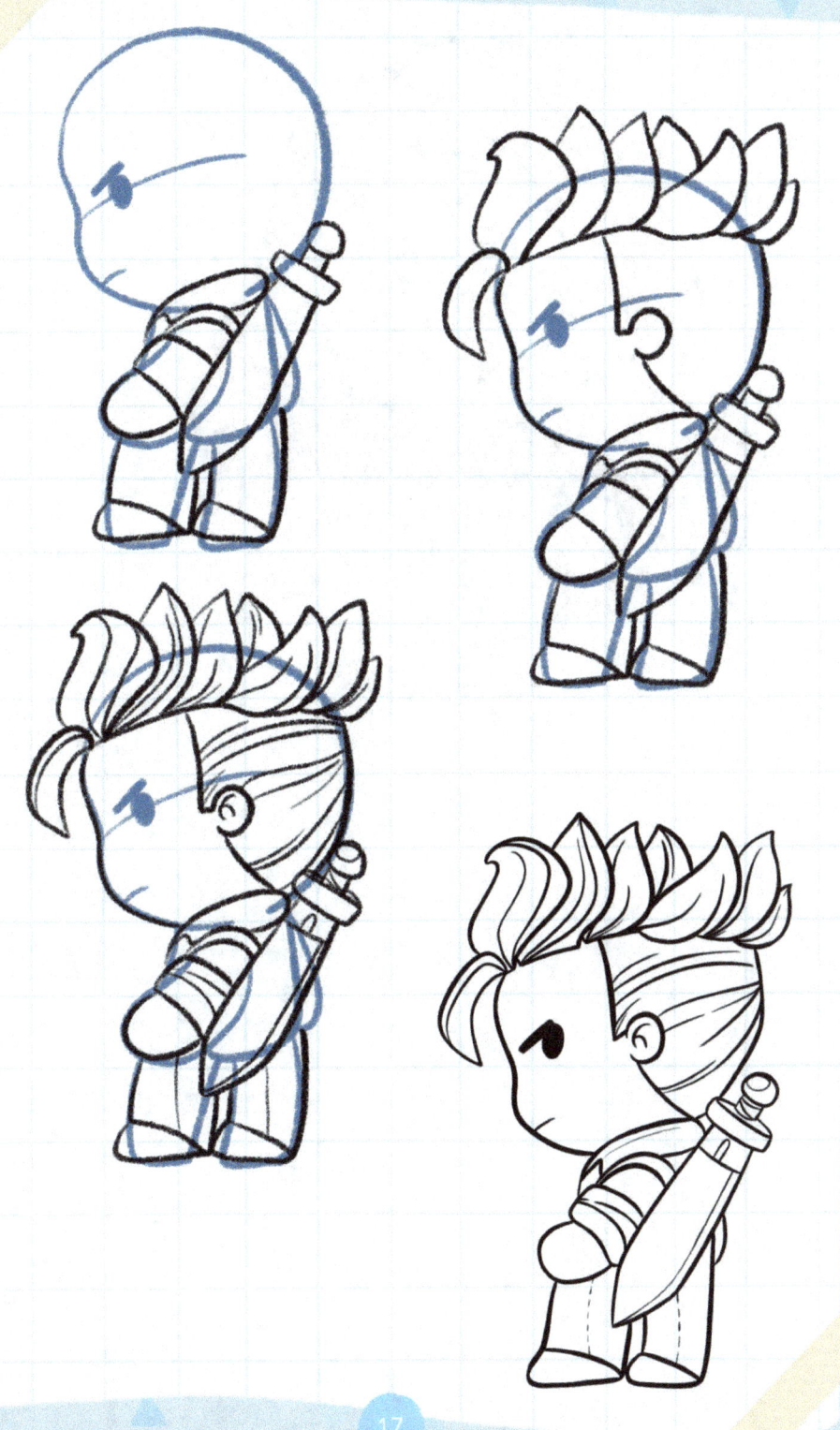

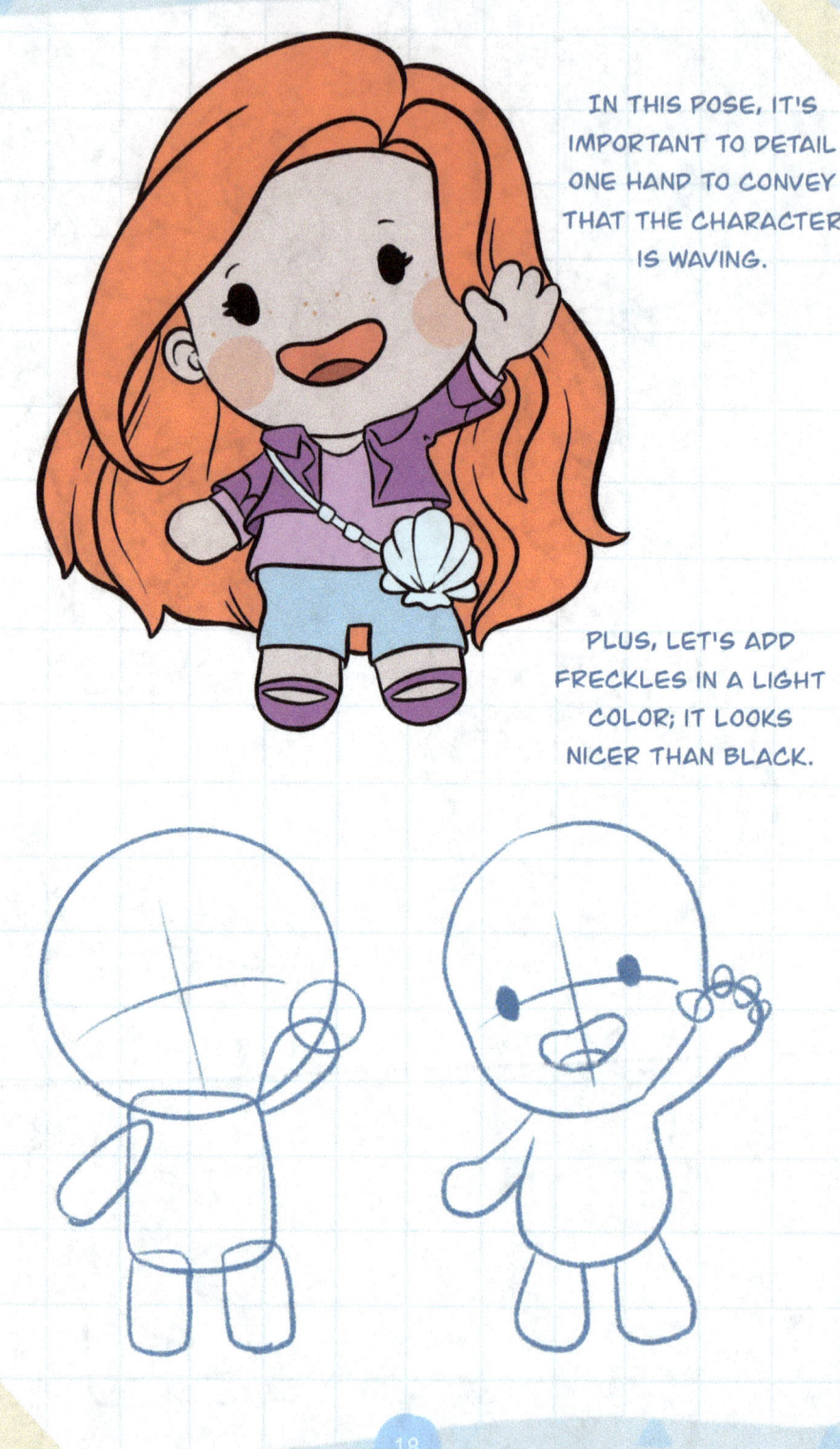

IN THIS POSE, IT'S IMPORTANT TO DETAIL ONE HAND TO CONVEY THAT THE CHARACTER IS WAVING.

PLUS, LET'S ADD FRECKLES IN A LIGHT COLOR; IT LOOKS NICER THAN BLACK.

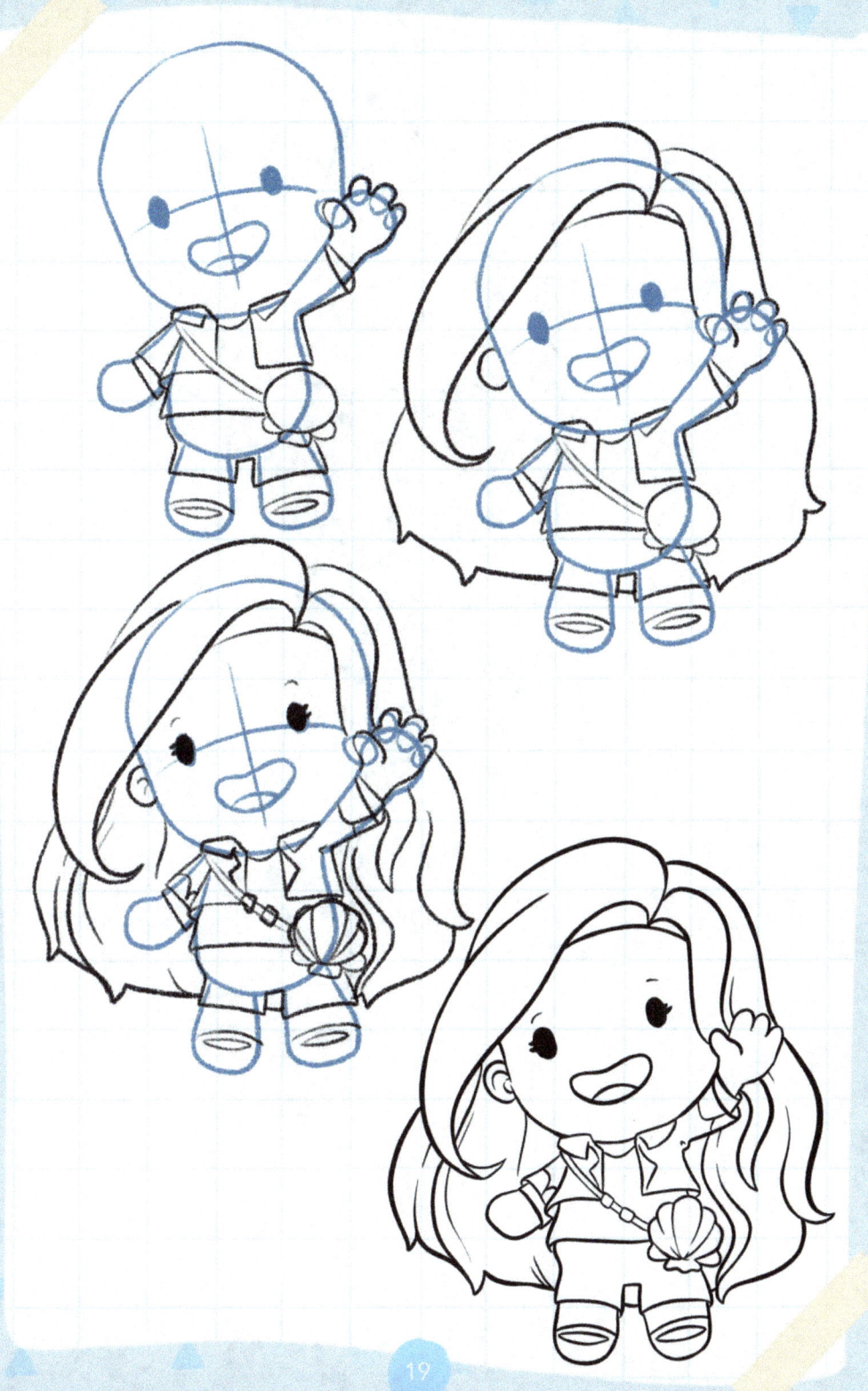

MANPU* SIGNS ARE USED TO ADD MORE EXPRESSIVENESS TO THE CHARACTERS, AND TODAY THEY ARE WELL-KNOWN AS EMOJIS.

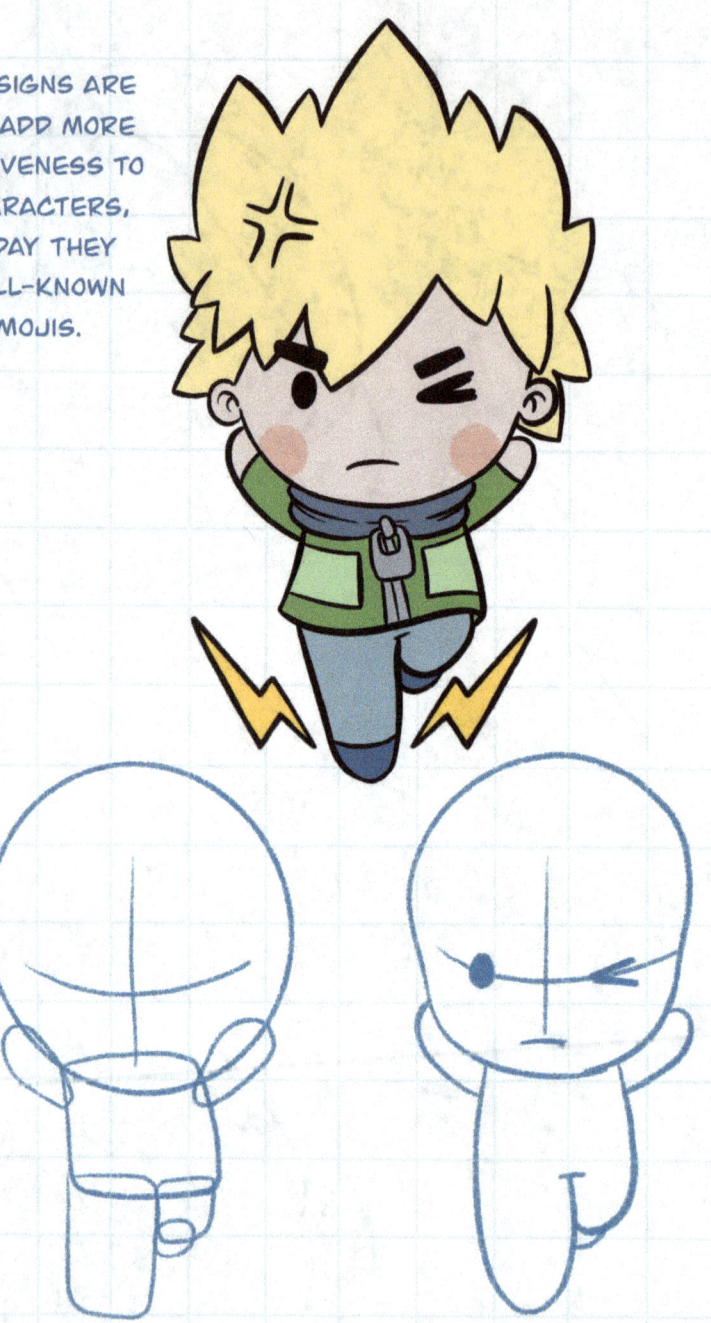

MANPU: A JAPANESE TERM FOR REPRESENTING EMOTIONS.

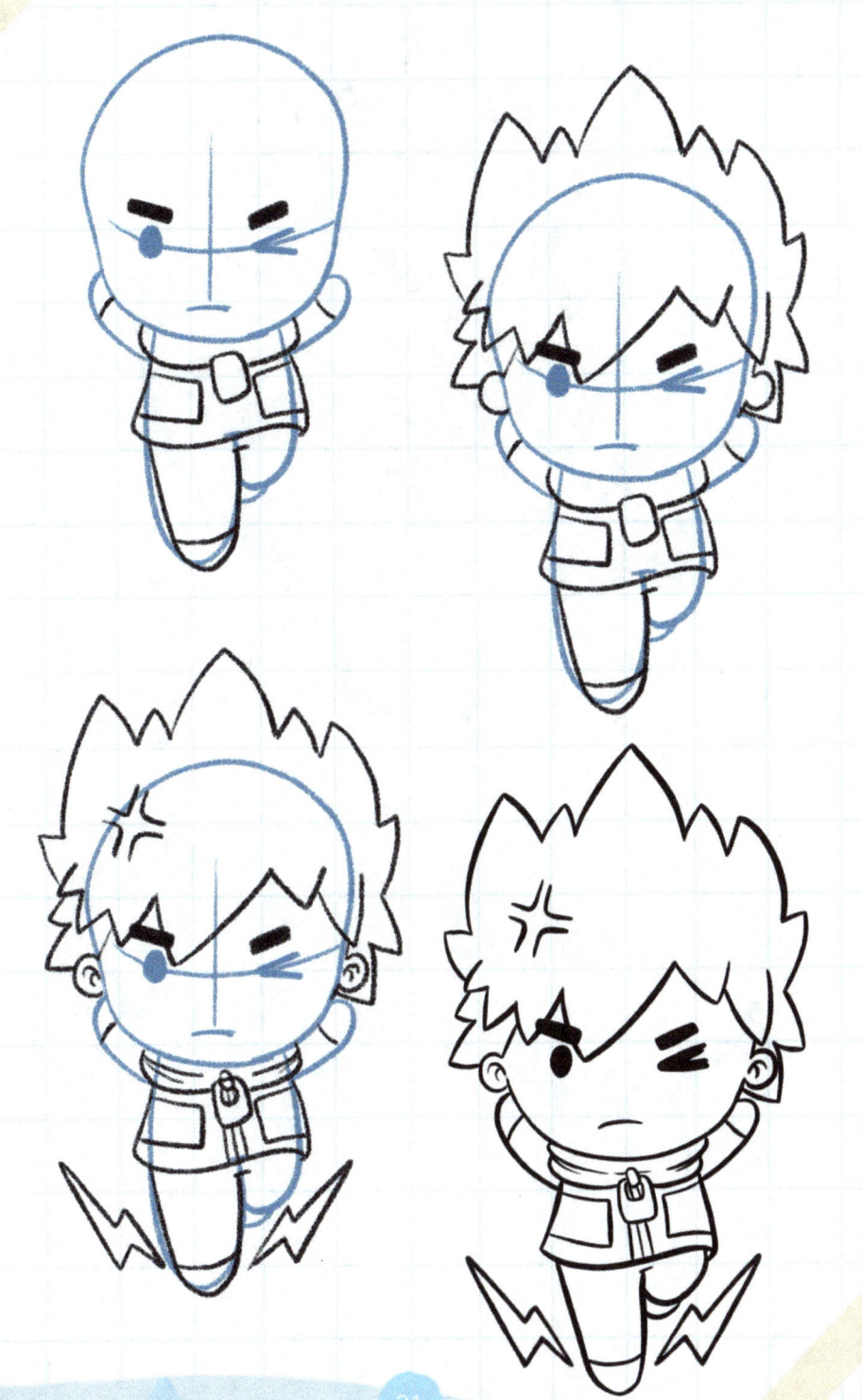

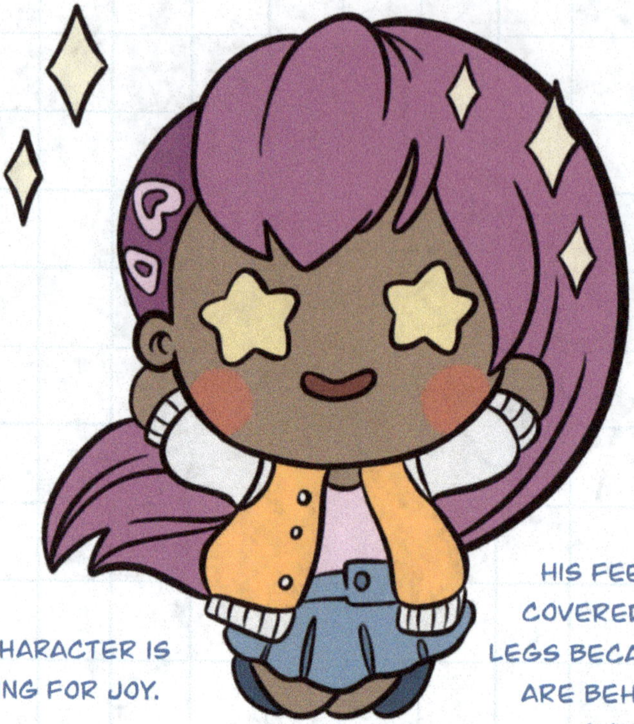

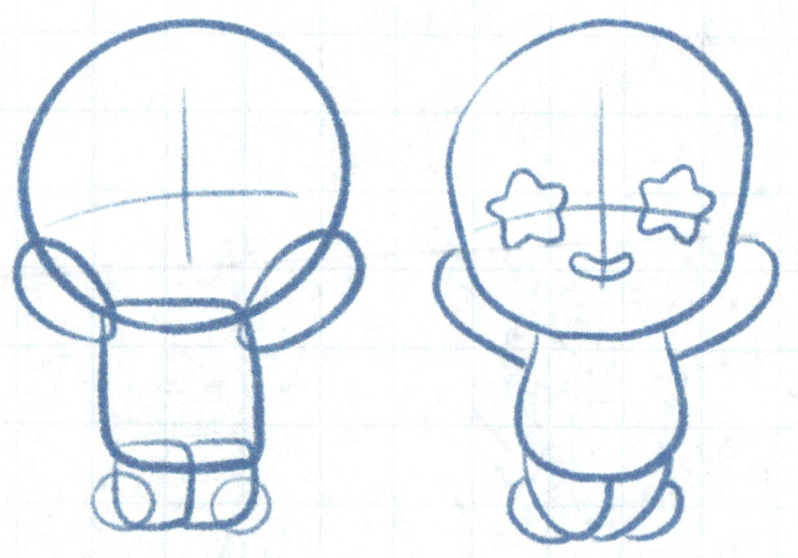

THIS CHARACTER IS JUMPING FOR JOY.

HIS FEET ARE COVERED BY HIS LEGS BECAUSE THEY ARE BEHIND THE FIGURE.

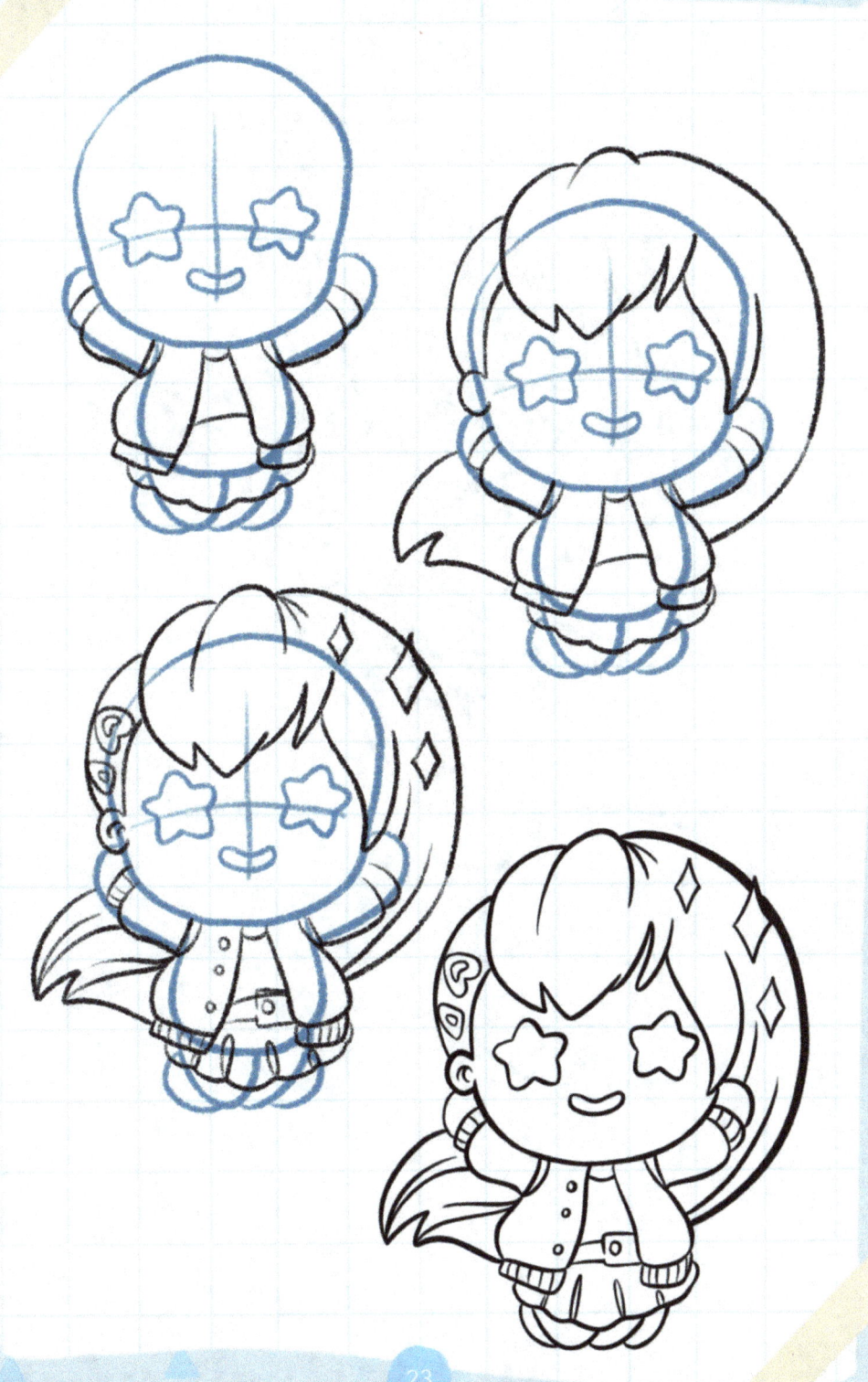

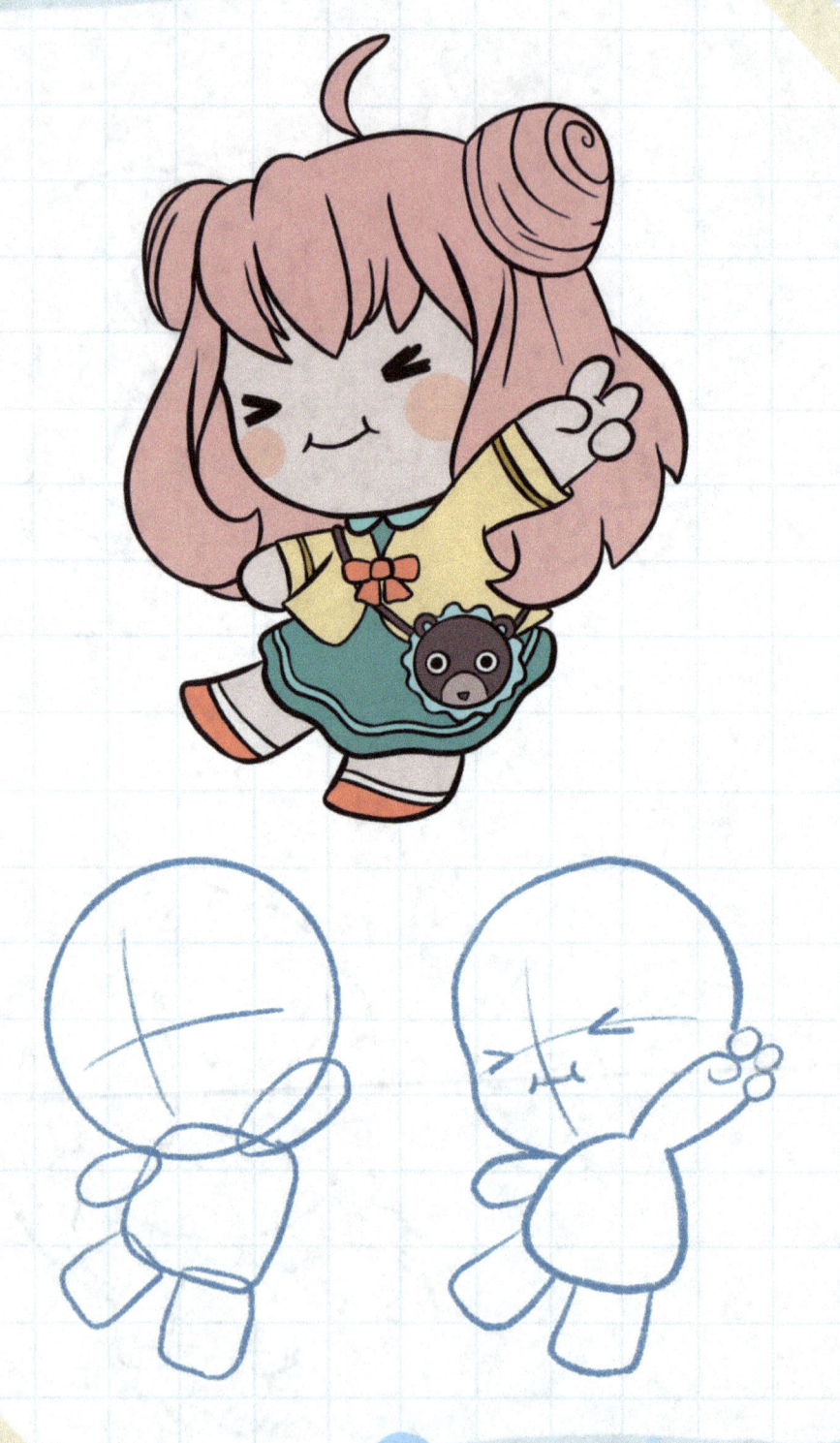

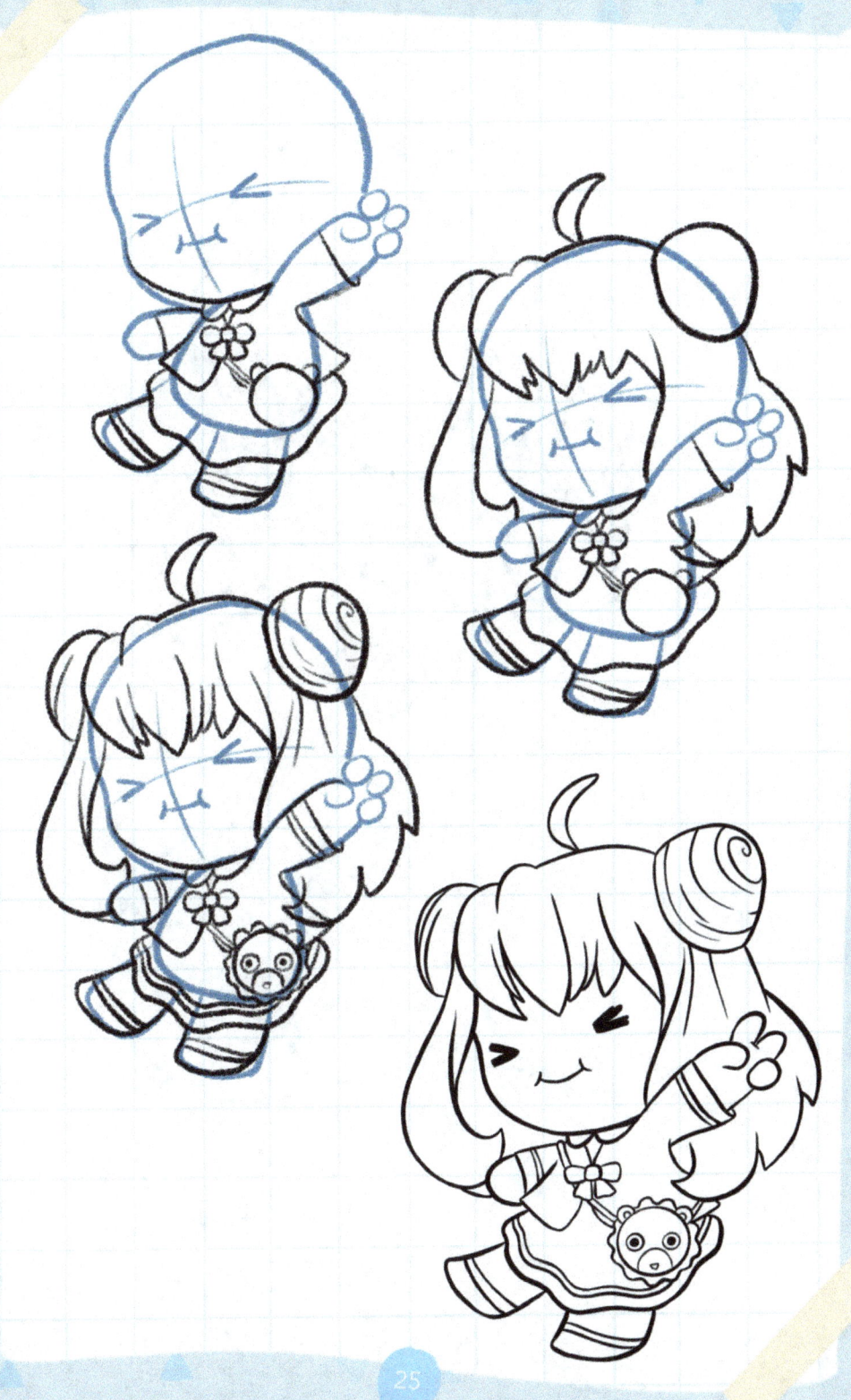

TO DRAW A KAWAII-
STYLE KISS, YOU
SHOULD DRAW A '3'
SHAPE AS THE
MOUTH

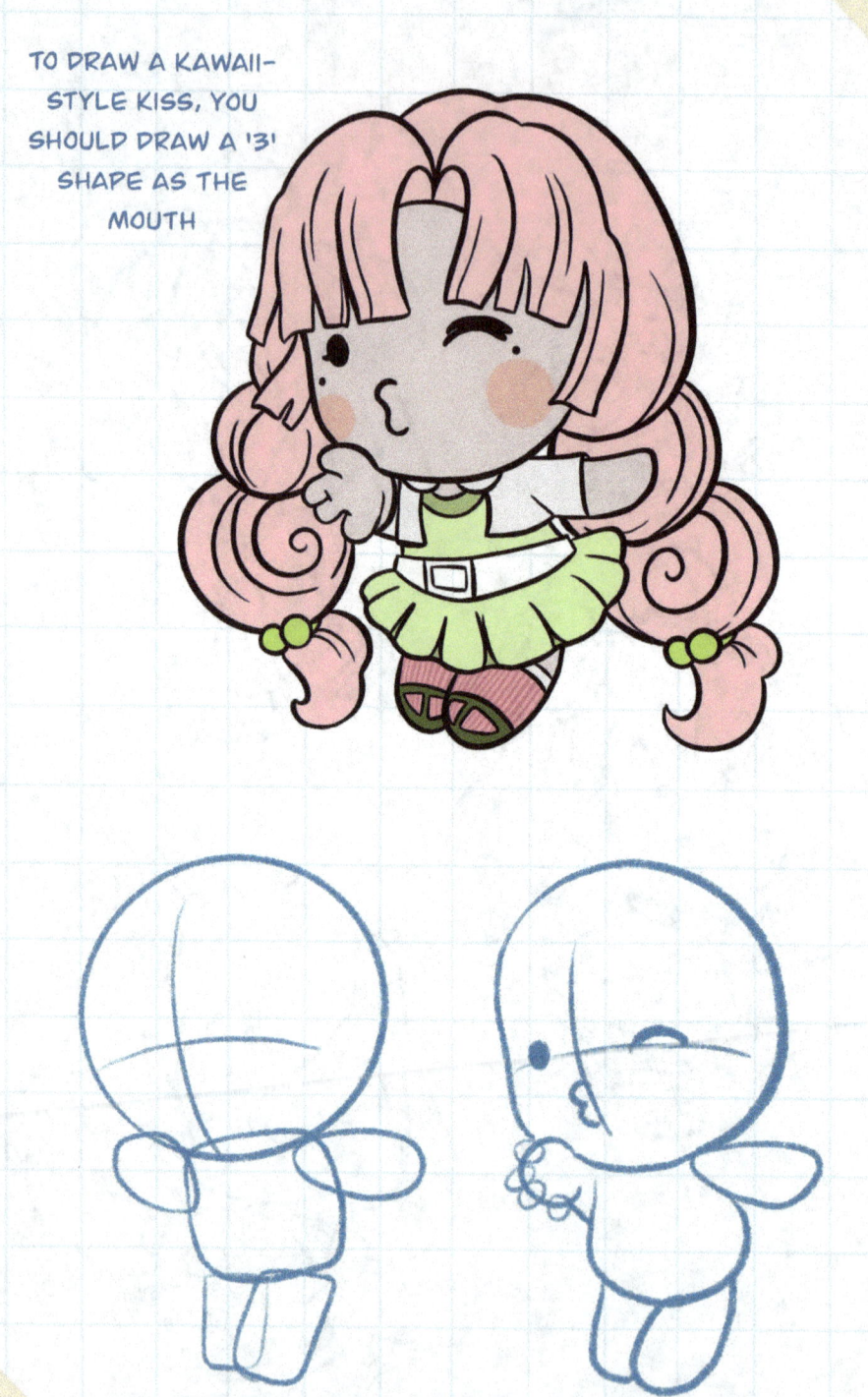

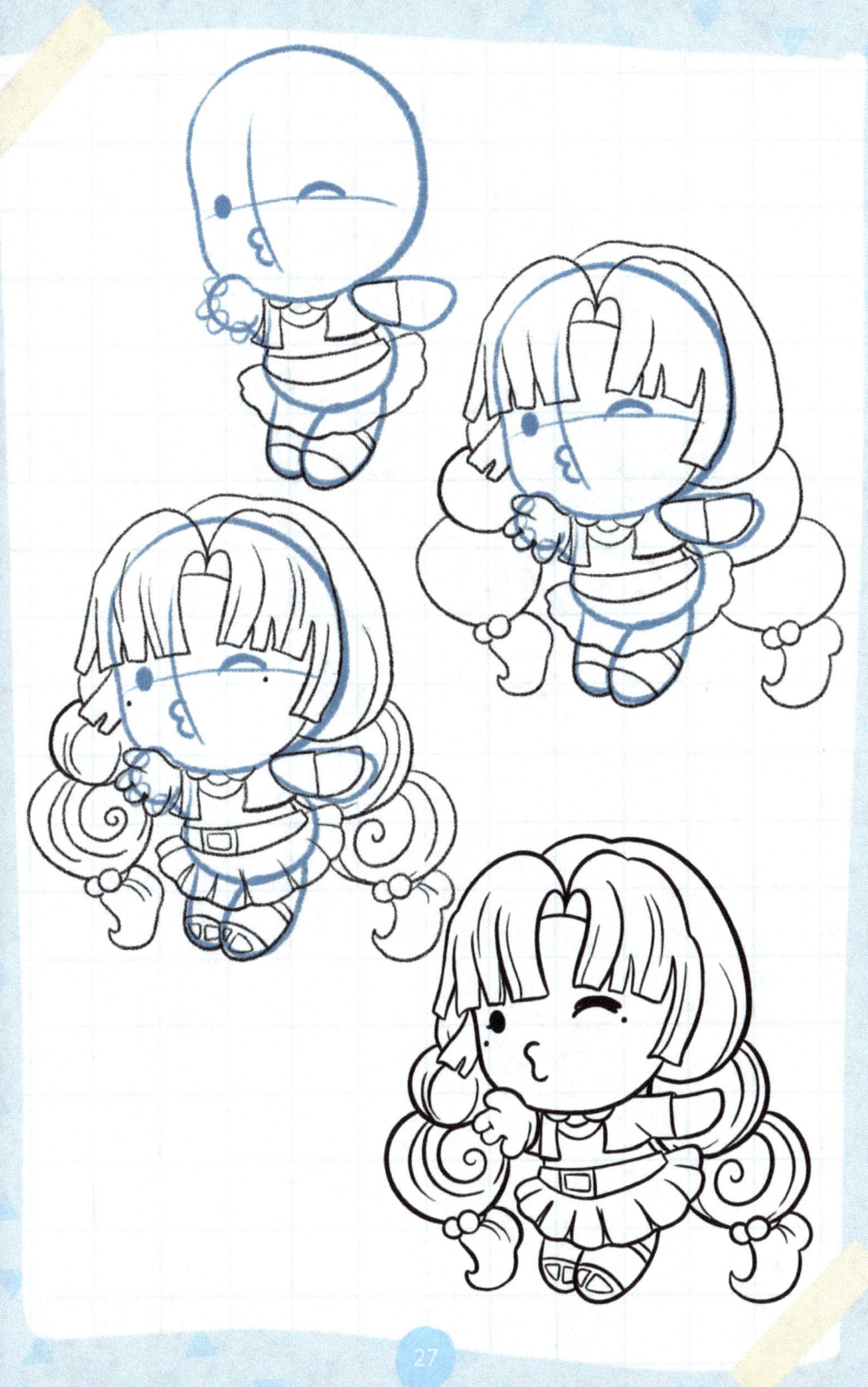

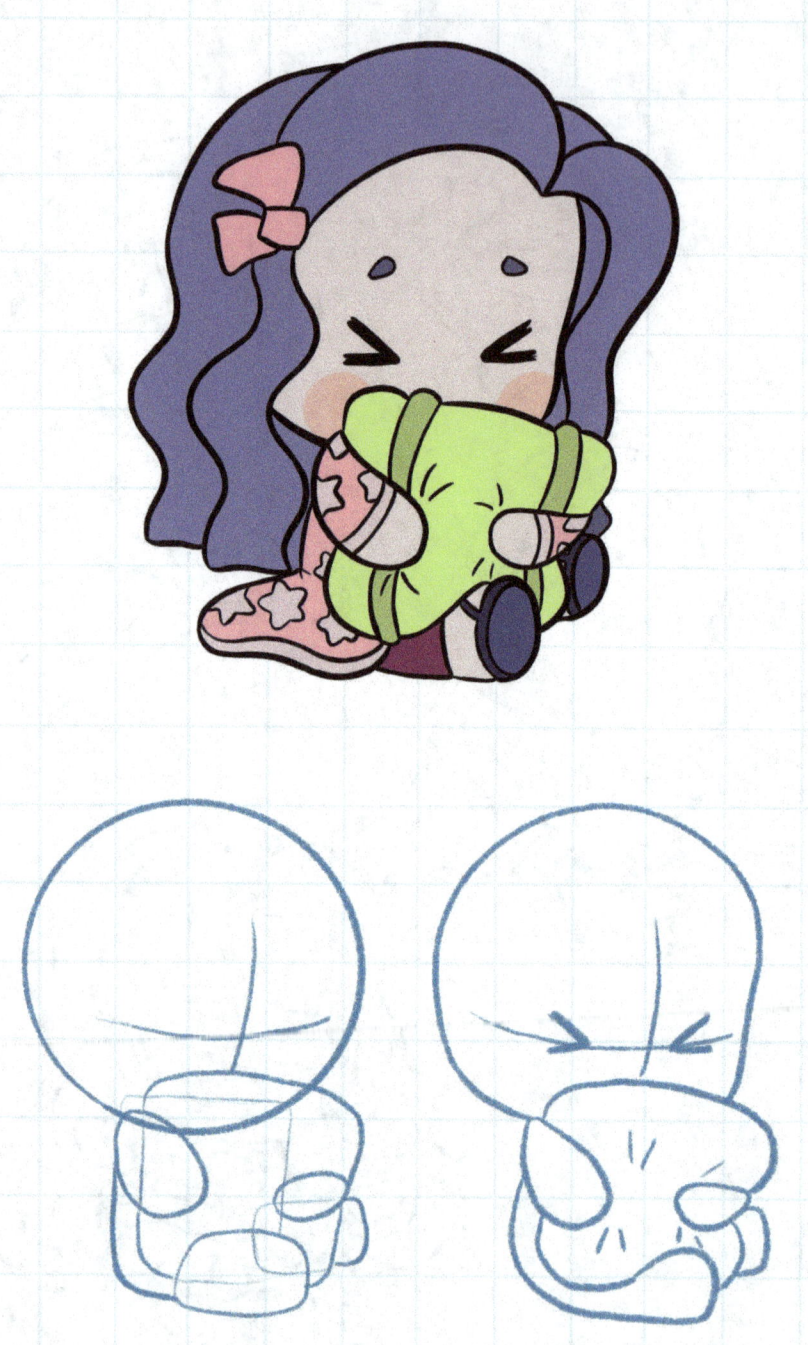

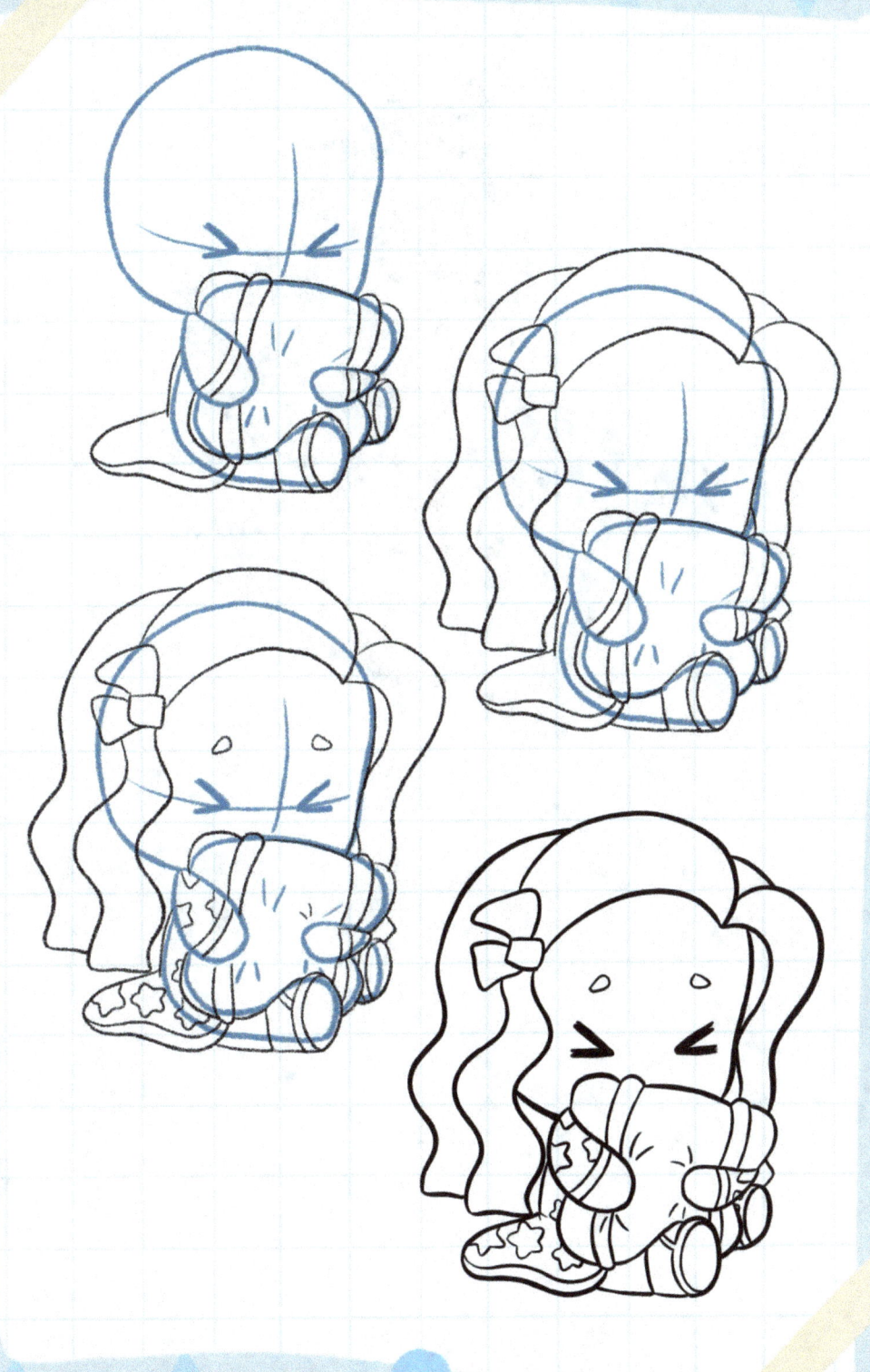

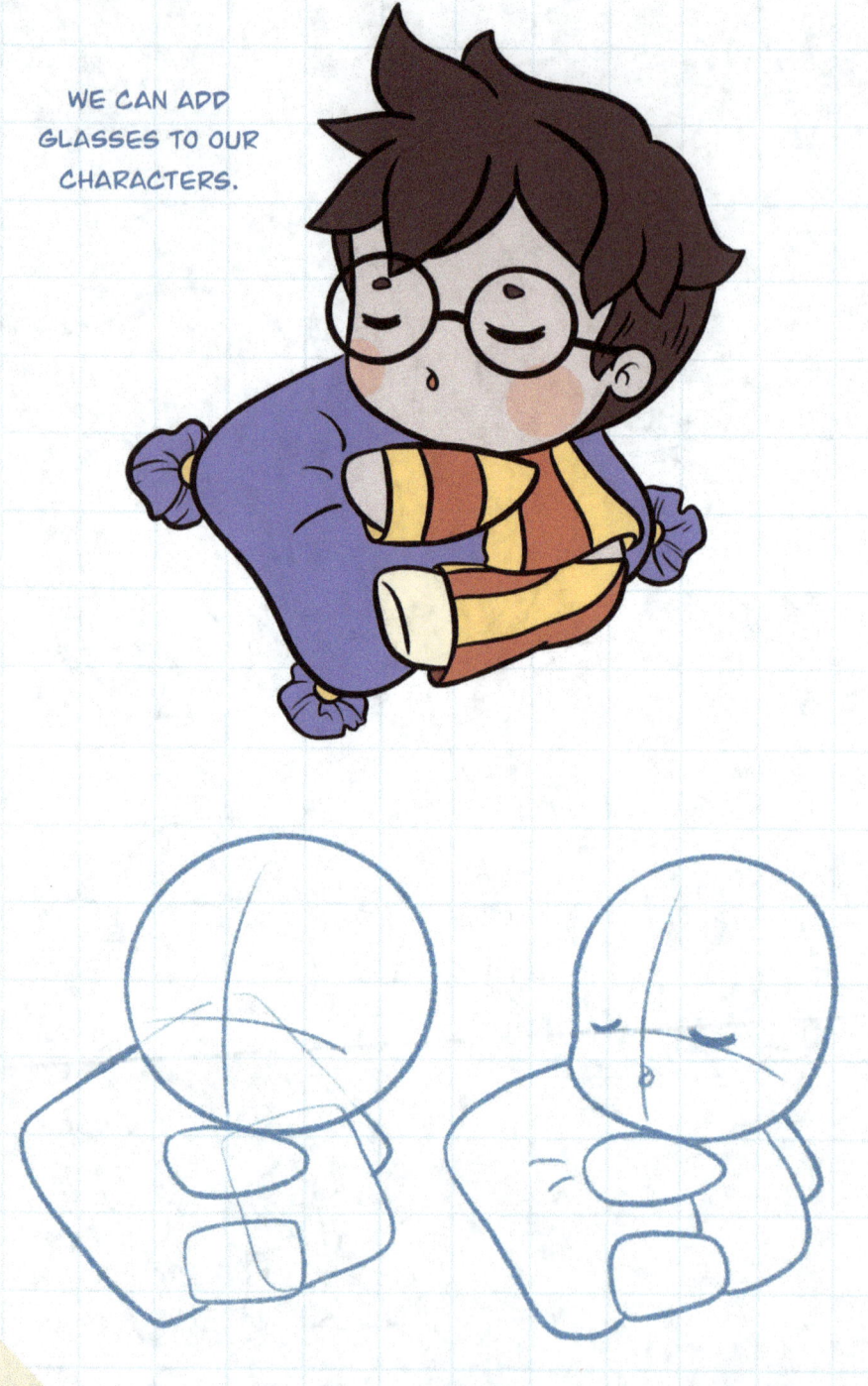

WE CAN ADD GLASSES TO OUR CHARACTERS.

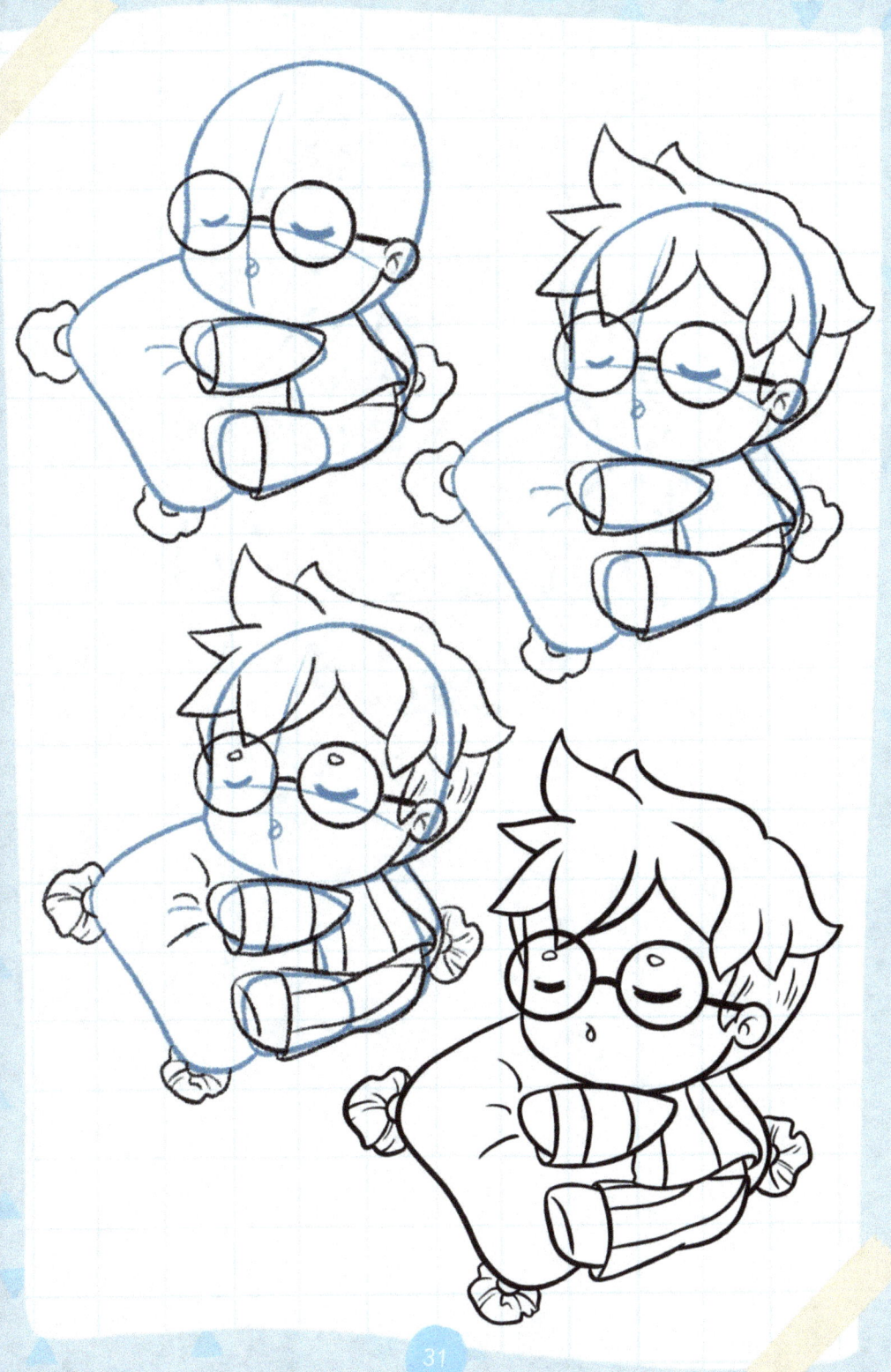

EVEN MORE
FASHIONABLE
GLASSES.

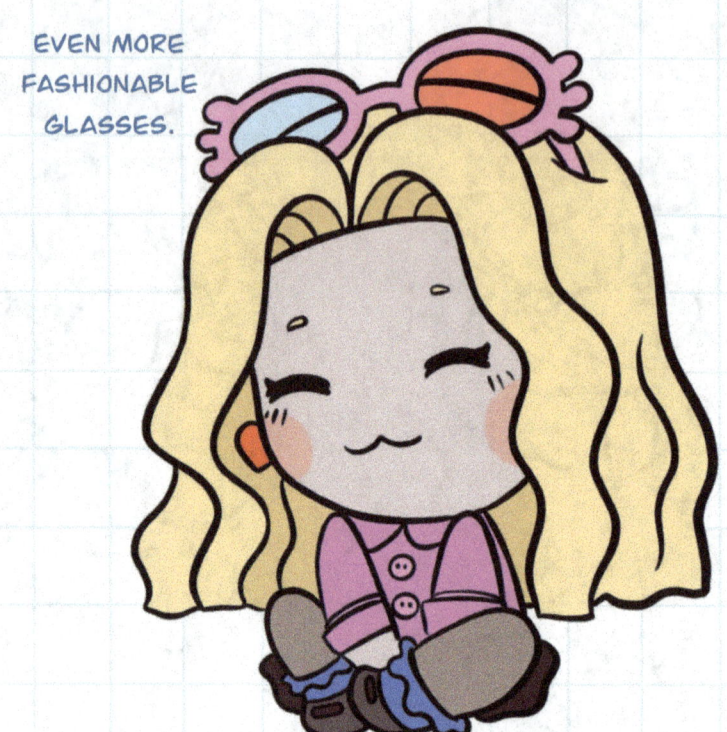

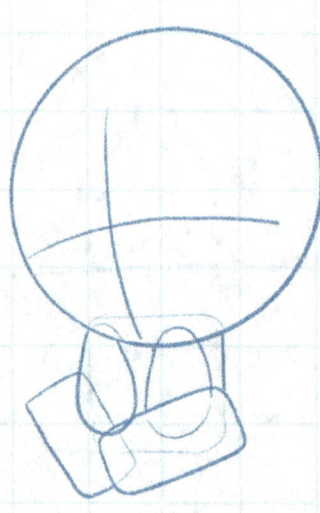

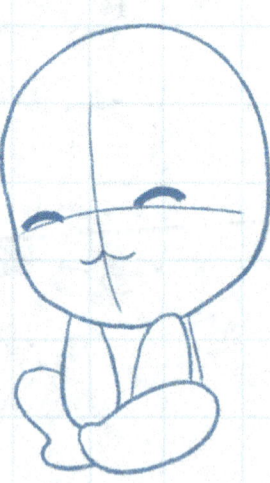

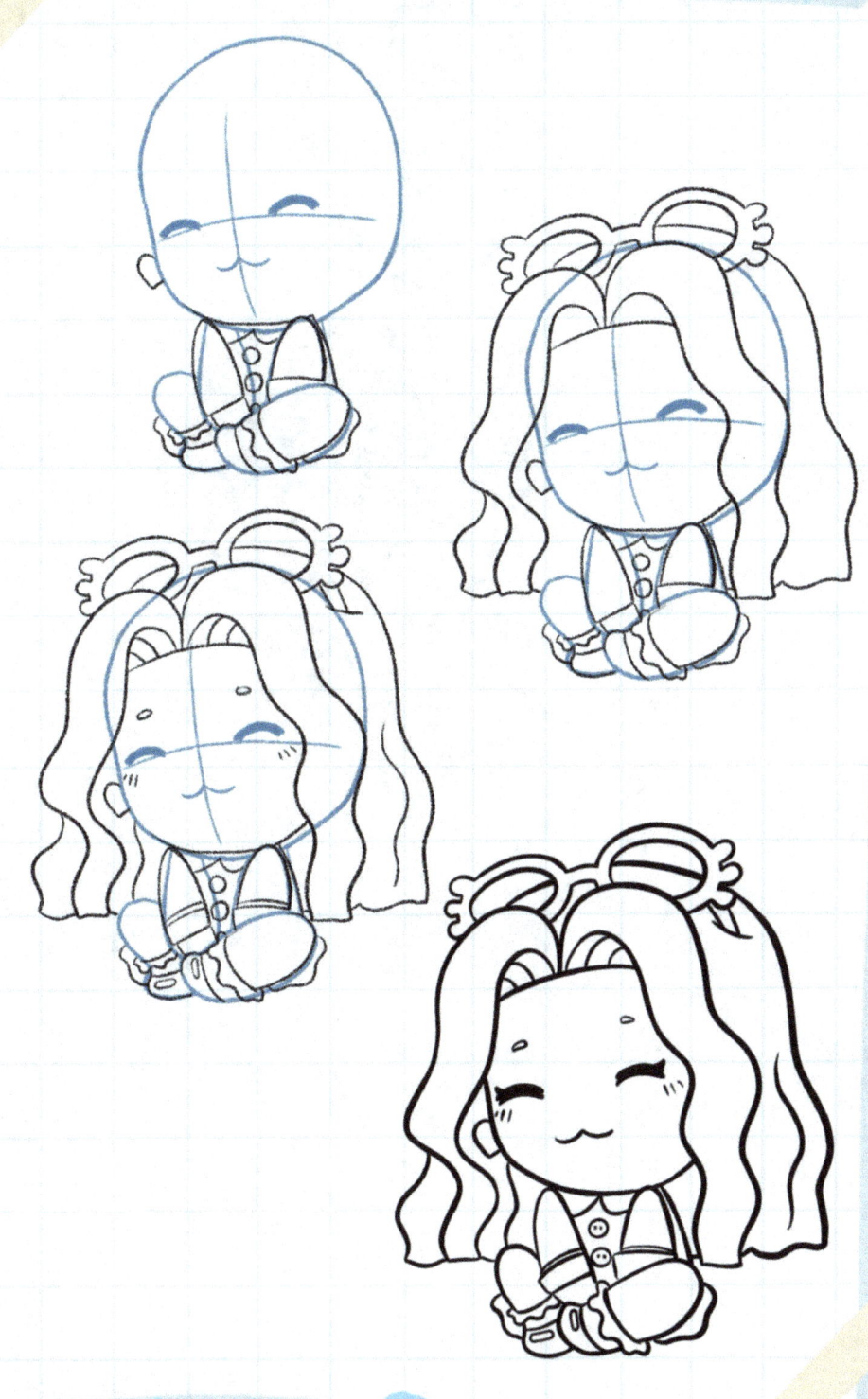

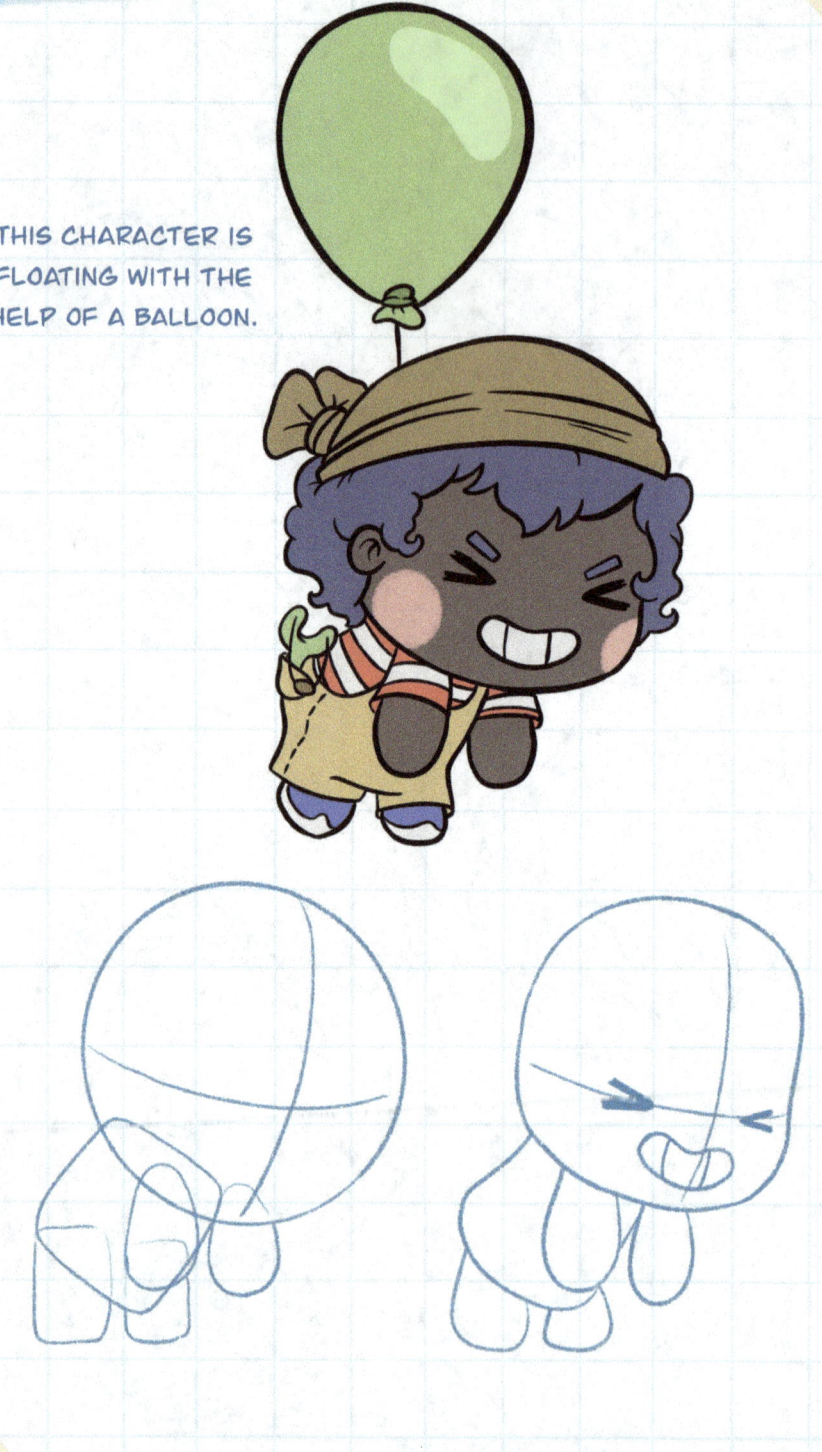

THIS CHARACTER IS FLOATING WITH THE HELP OF A BALLOON.

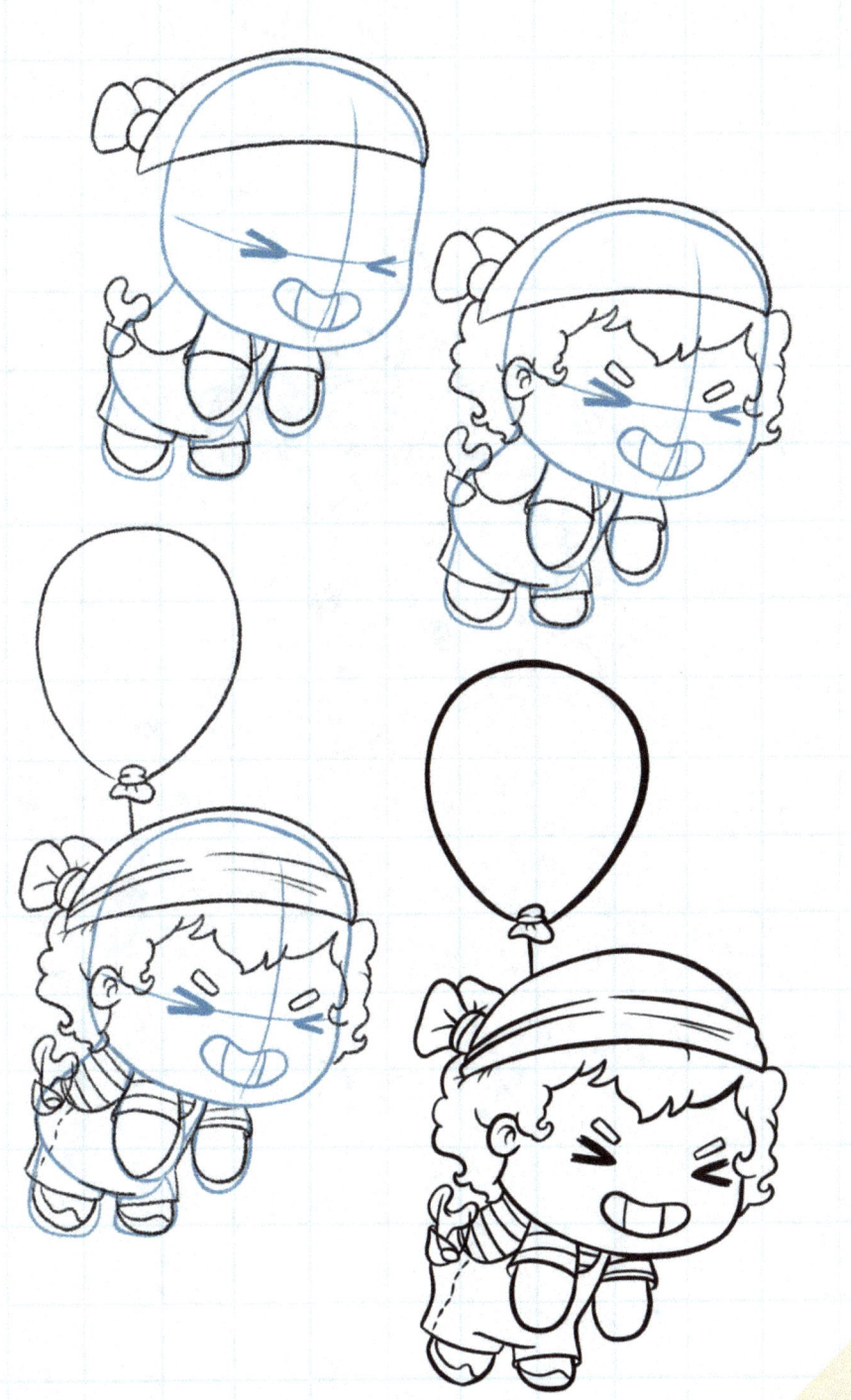

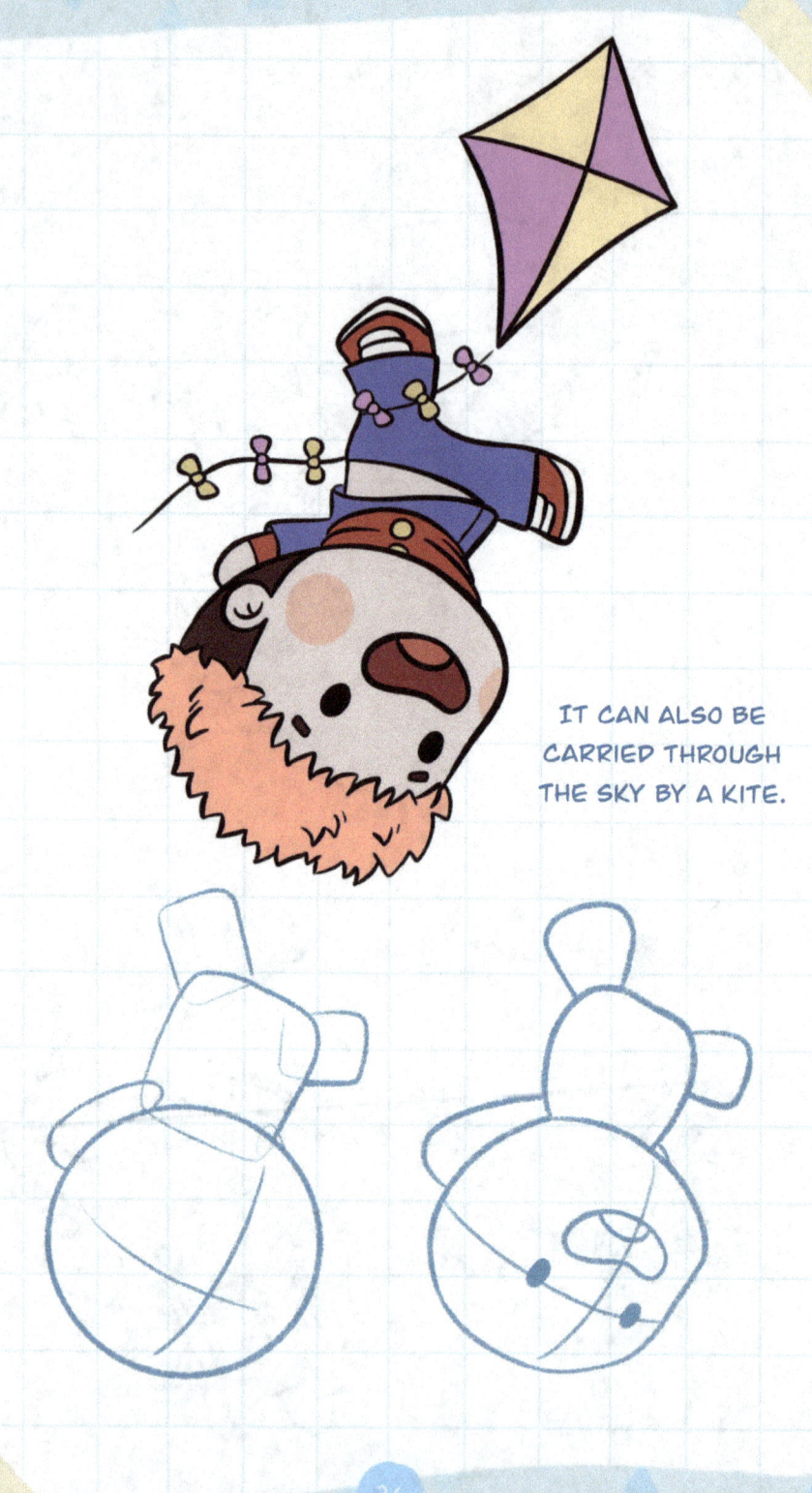

IT CAN ALSO BE
CARRIED THROUGH
THE SKY BY A KITE.

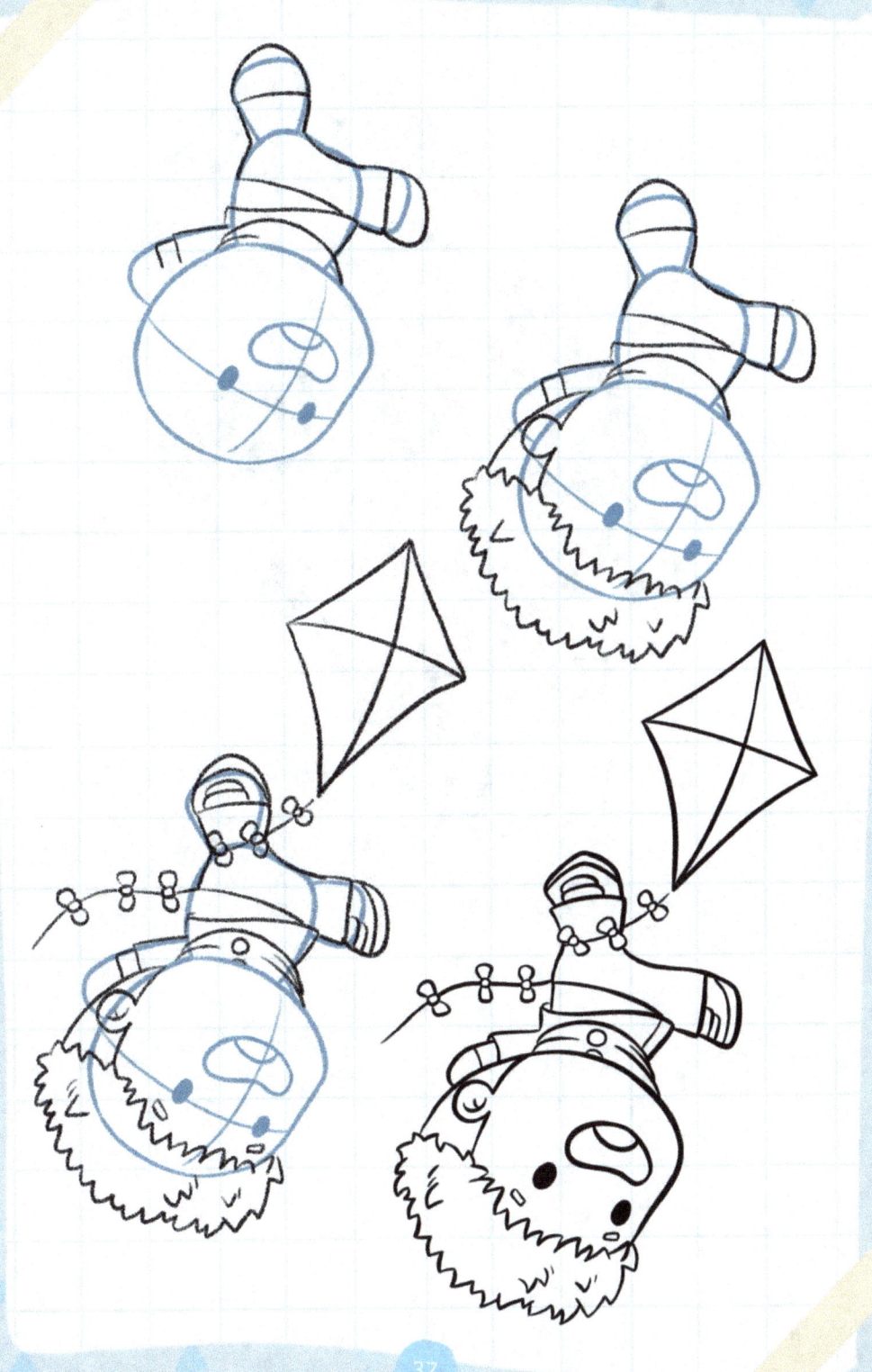

OR GLIDING THROUGH
THE SKY WITH AN
UMBRELLA.

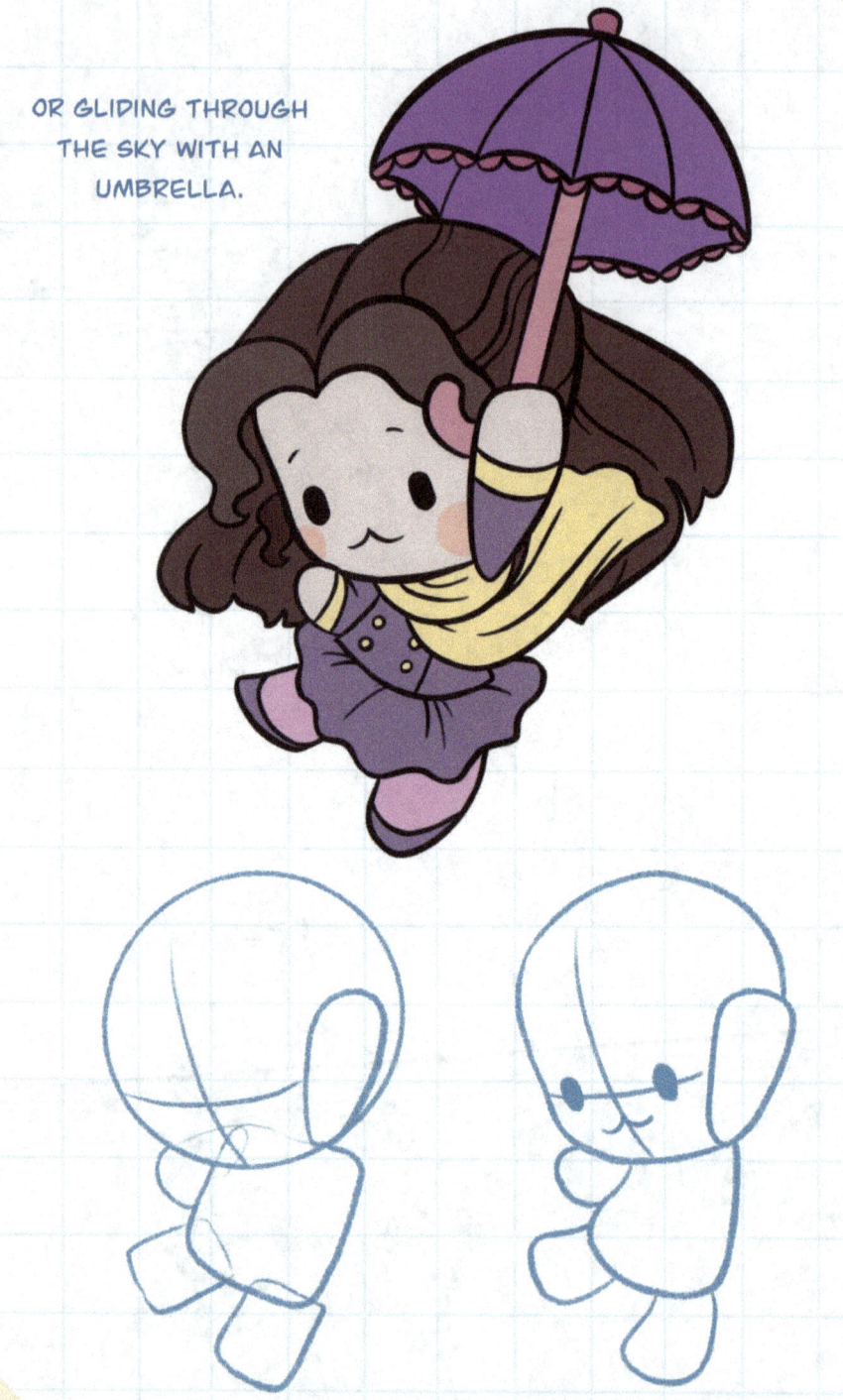

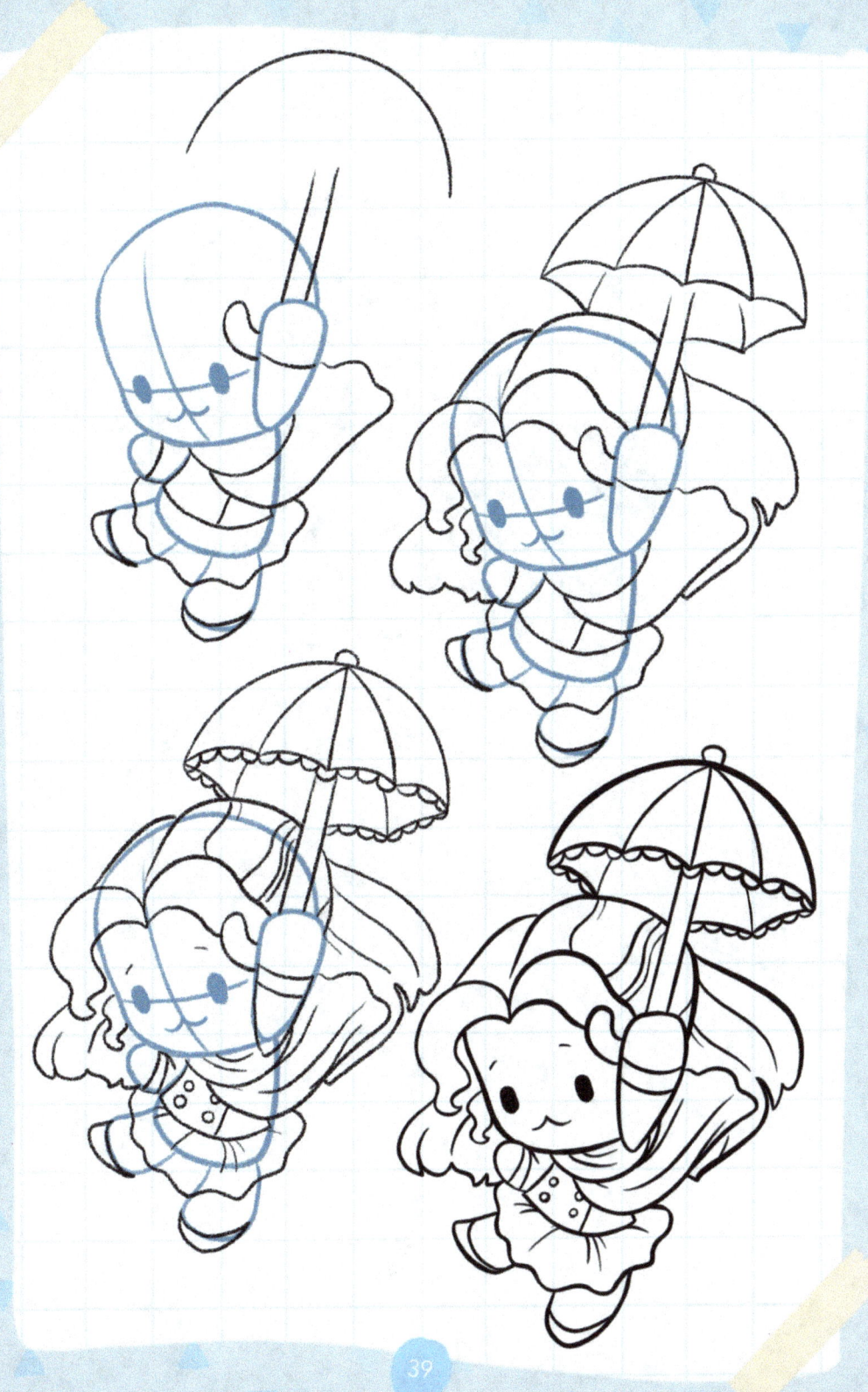

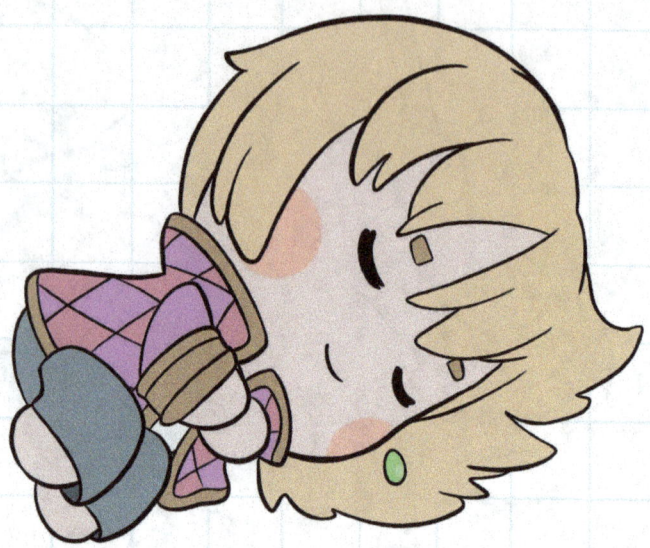

IT'S VERY CUTE TO DEPICT YOUR CHARACTER SLEEPING.

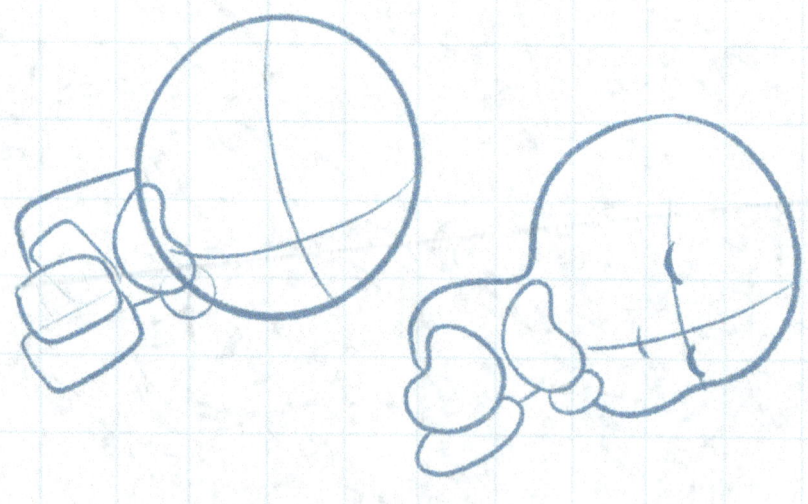

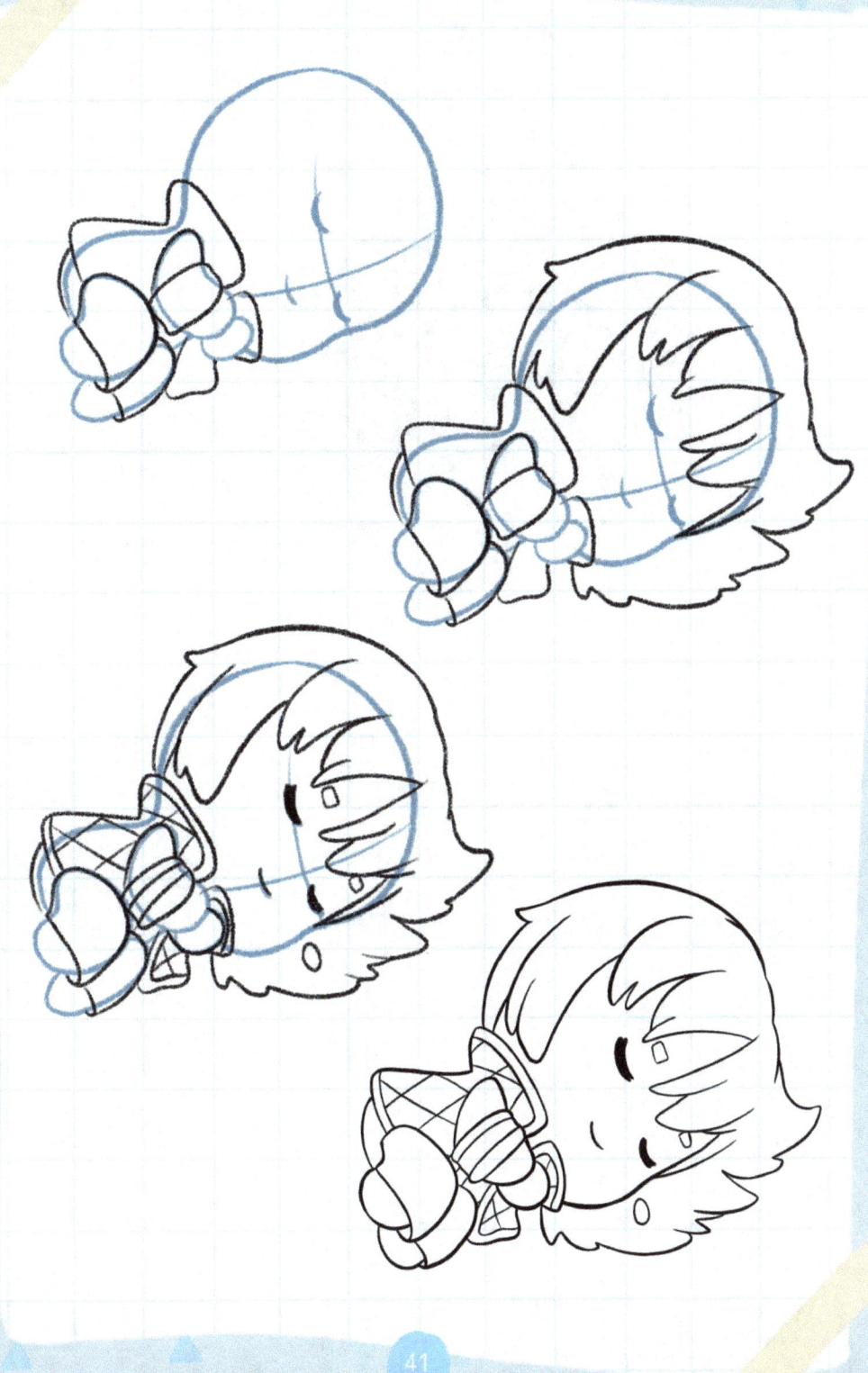

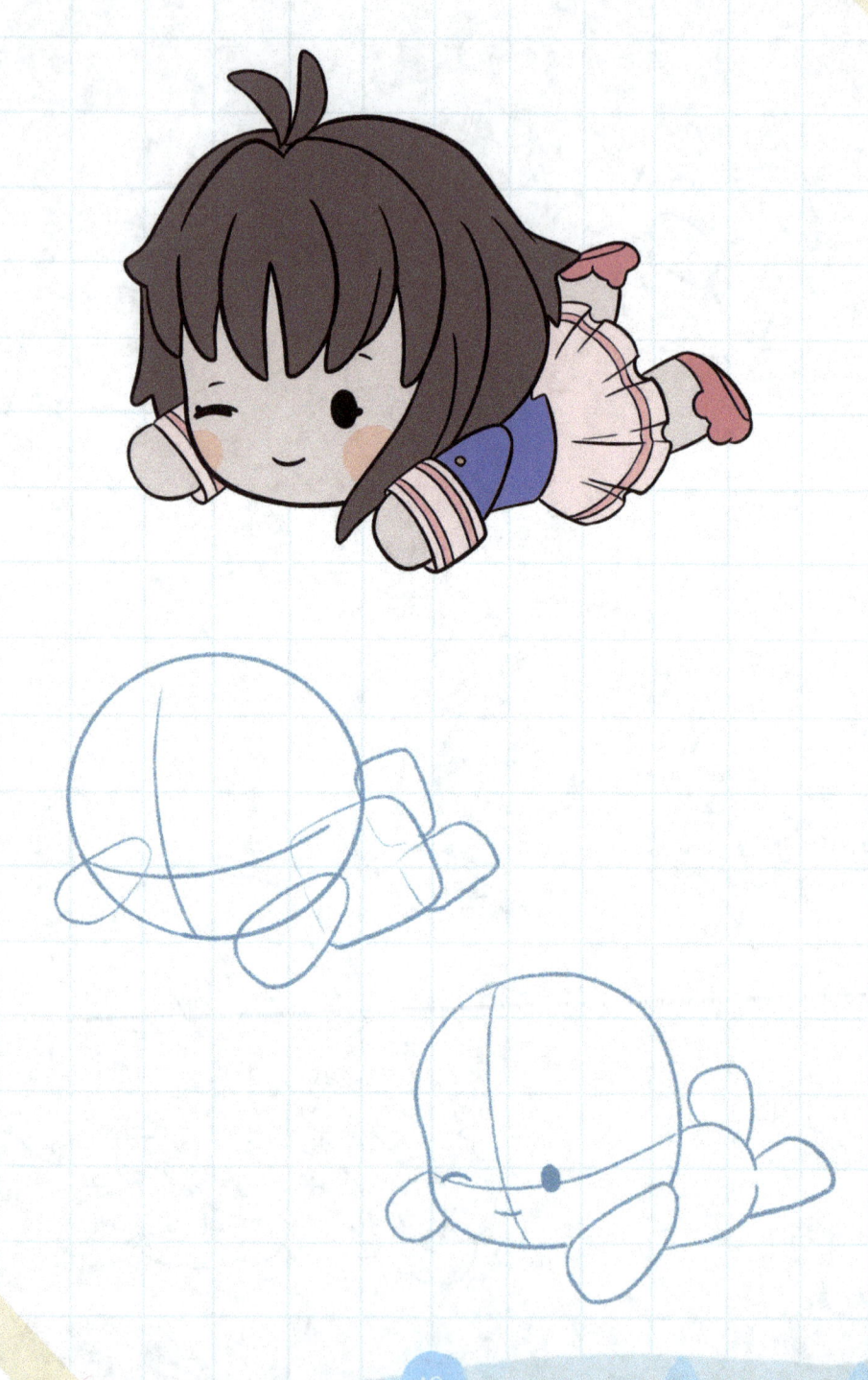

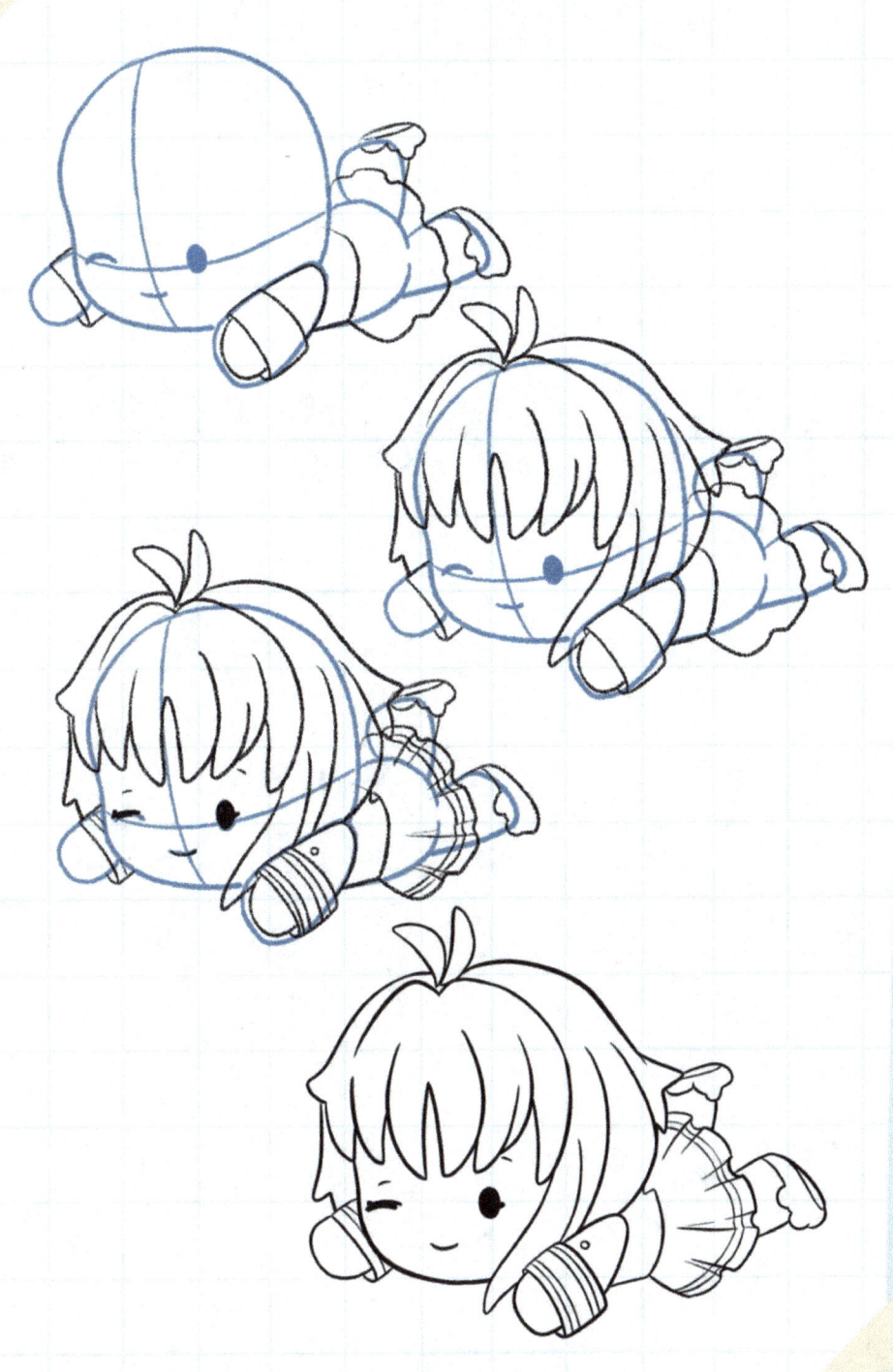

ANIMALS

LET'S LEARN HOW TO CREATE SUPER CUTE KAWAII ANIMALS. THANKS
TO THE PREVIOUS LESSONS, IT'S GOING TO BE VERY EASY FOR US.

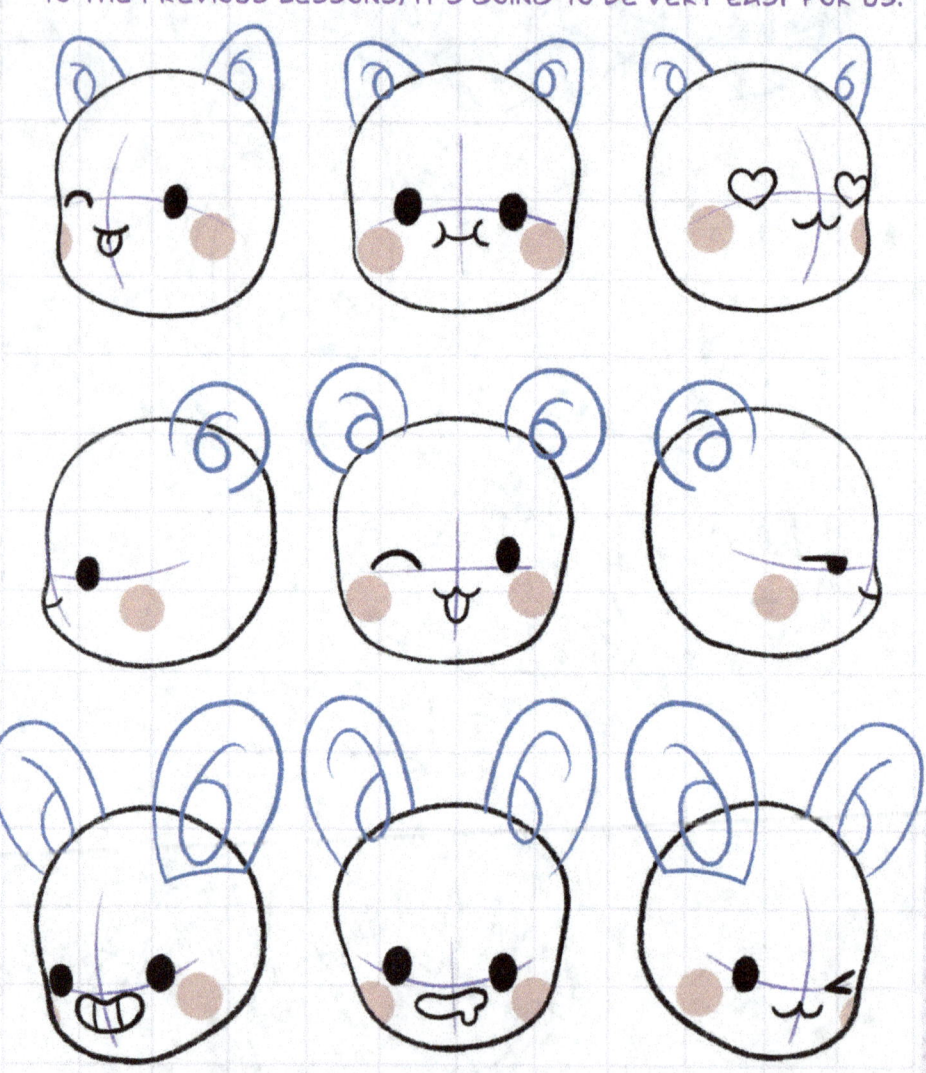

ADD YOUR FAVORITE EARS TO START. AS YOU CAN SEE,
THE INSIDE IS A '6' AND UPSIDE DOWN.

ANIMAL BODIES

THE STEP-BY-STEP PROCESS FOR CREATING THE BODY OF THE ANIMALS IS AN EXCELLENT WAY TO LEARN AND ADAPT IT TO DIFFERENT SPECIES.

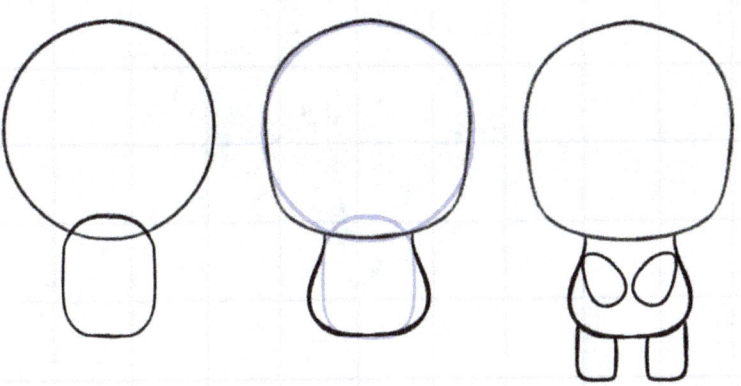

ADAPTING THE LIMBS TO THE ANIMAL SPECIES YOU'RE DRAWING IS ESSENTIAL TO ACHIEVE AN AUTHENTIC AND KAWAII LOOK.

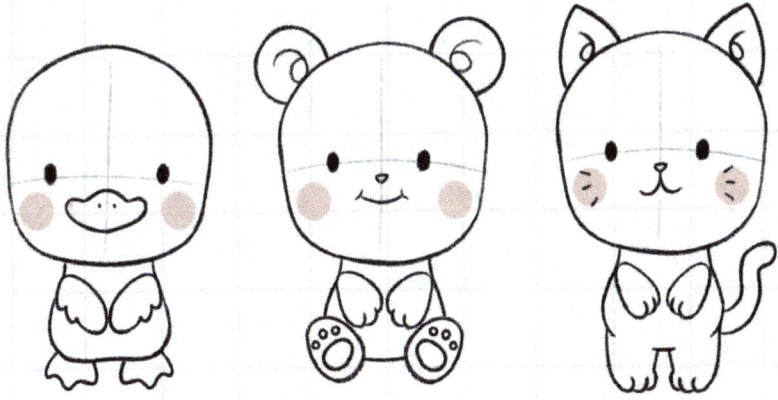

DON'T WORRY, WE'RE GOING TO PRACTICE MANY DIFFERENT STYLES WITH OUR LIST OF POSES.

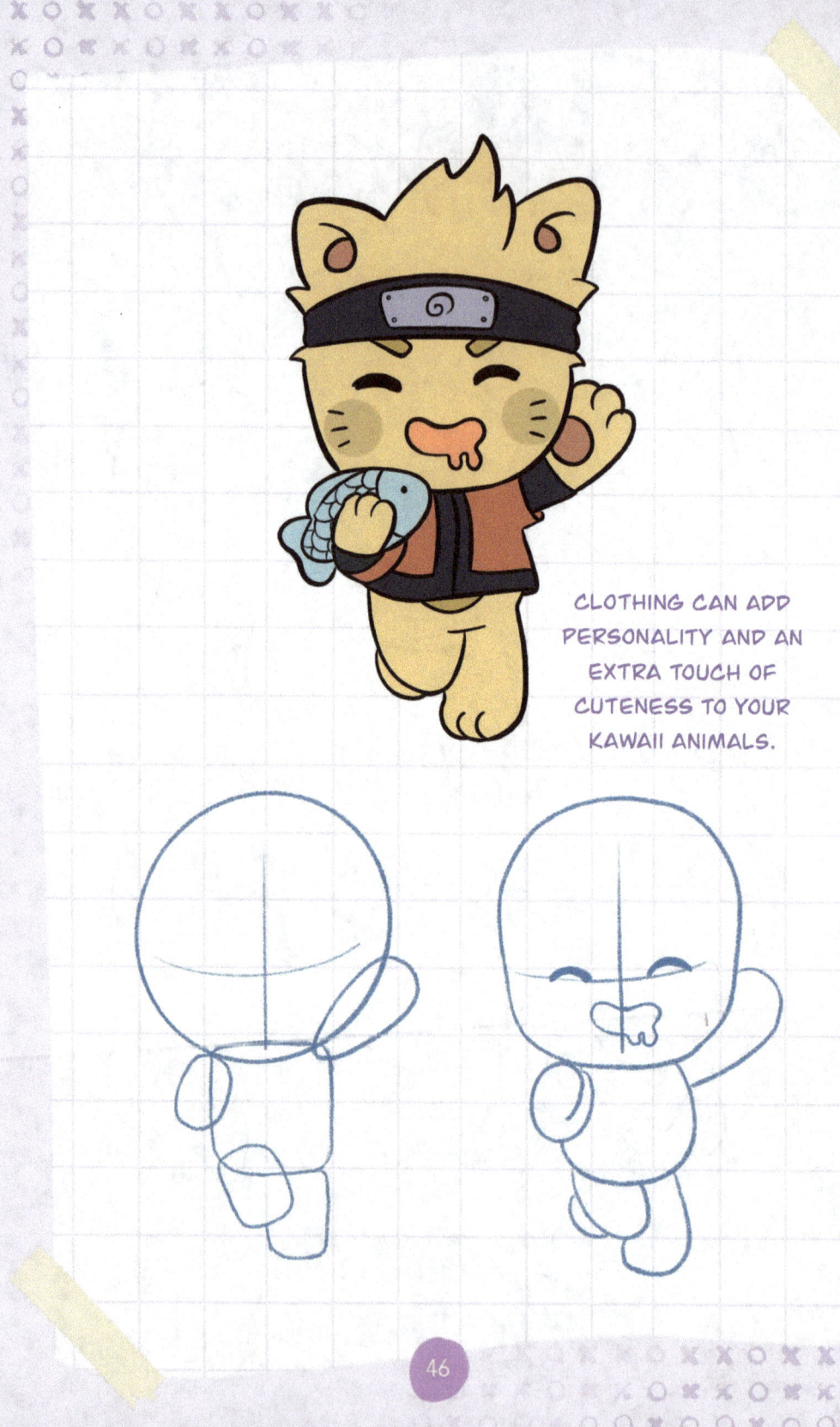

CLOTHING CAN ADD
PERSONALITY AND AN
EXTRA TOUCH OF
CUTENESS TO YOUR
KAWAII ANIMALS.

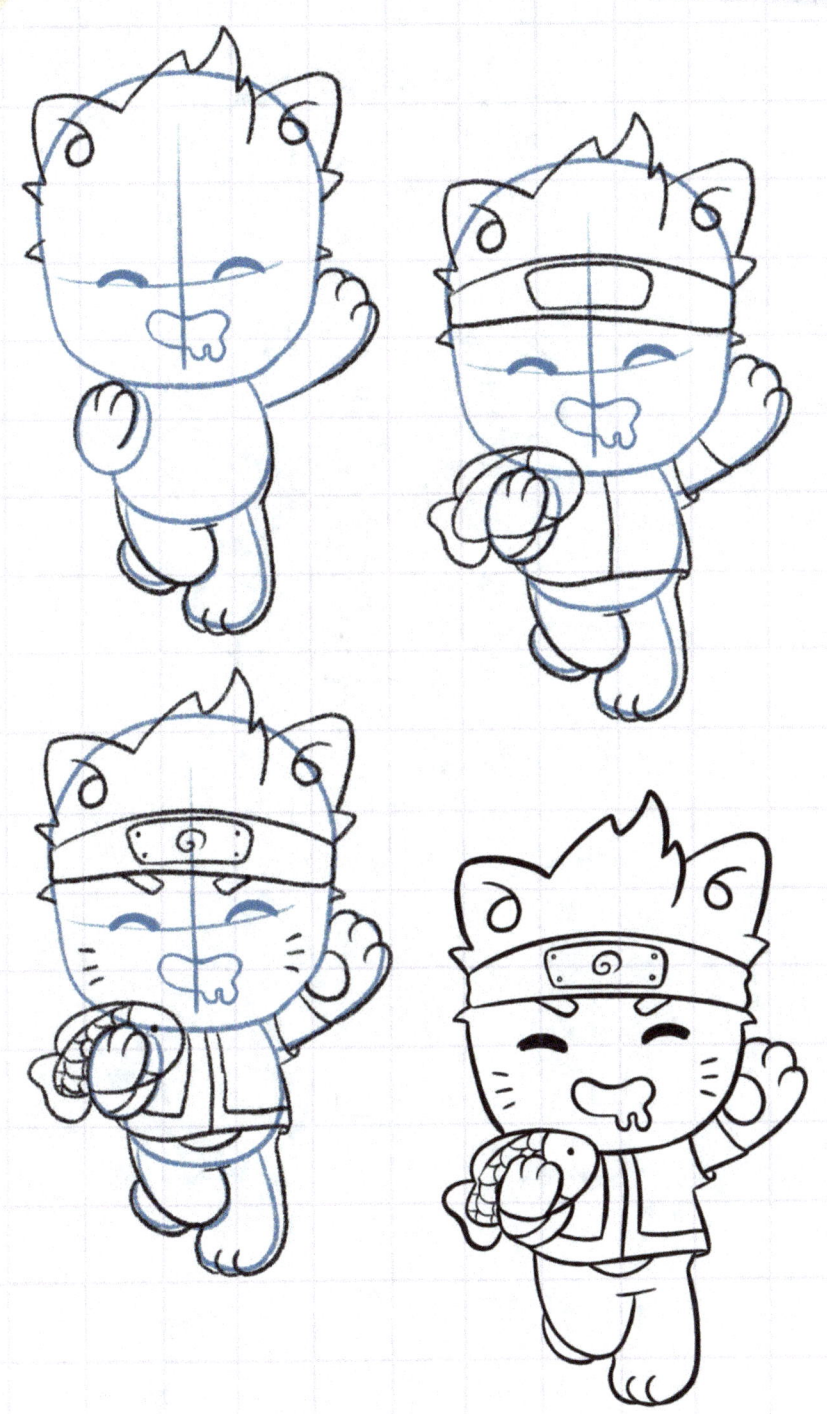

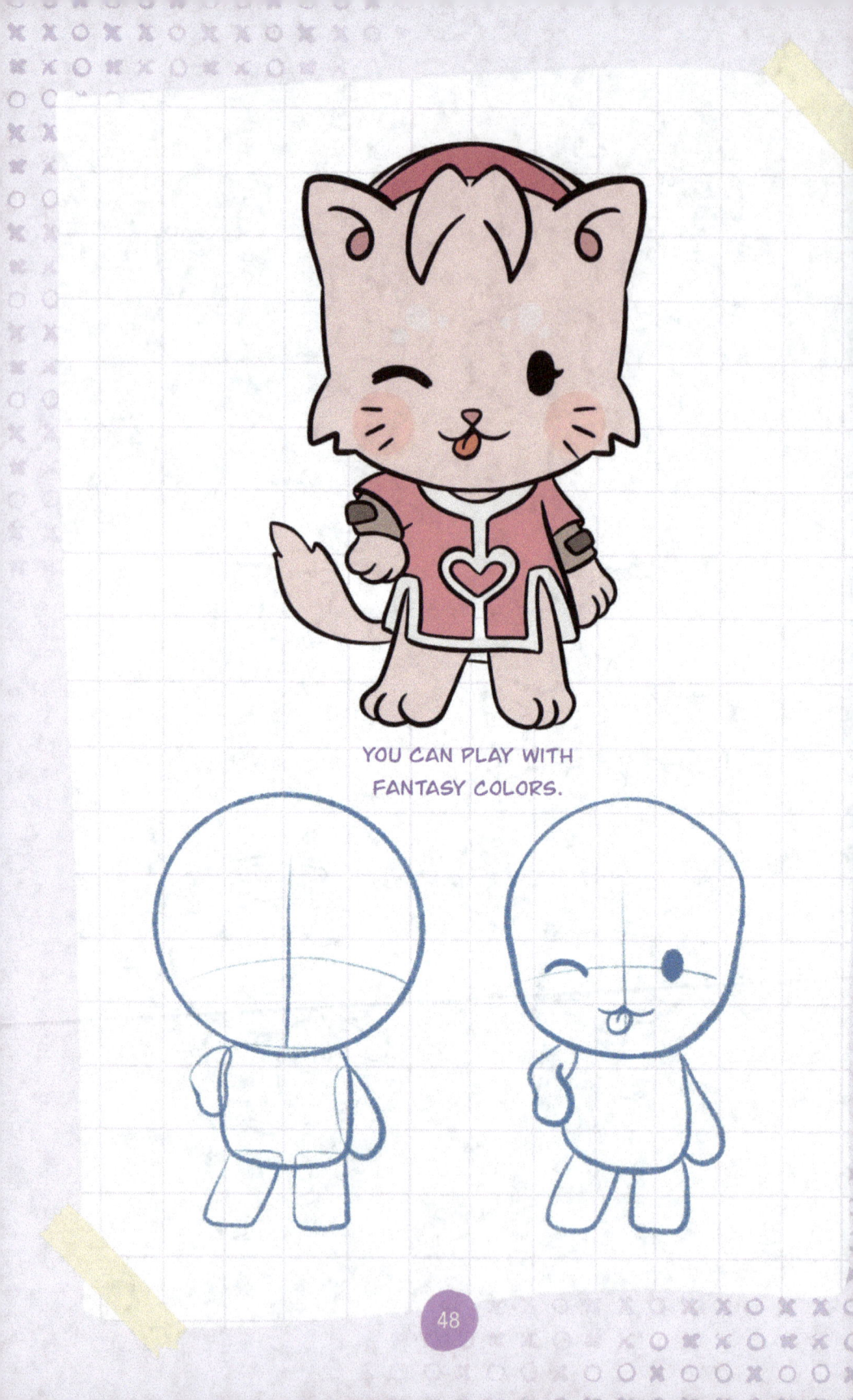

YOU CAN PLAY WITH
FANTASY COLORS.

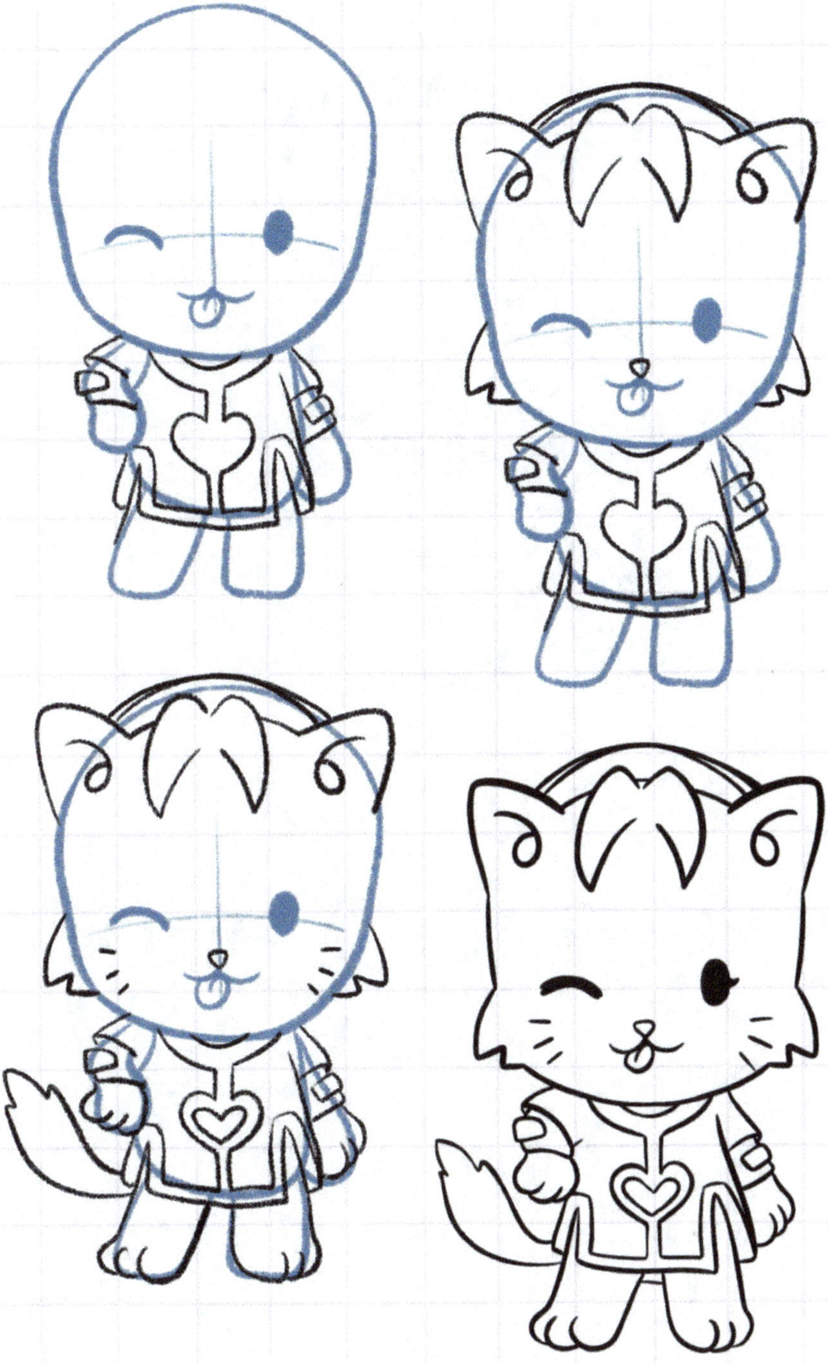

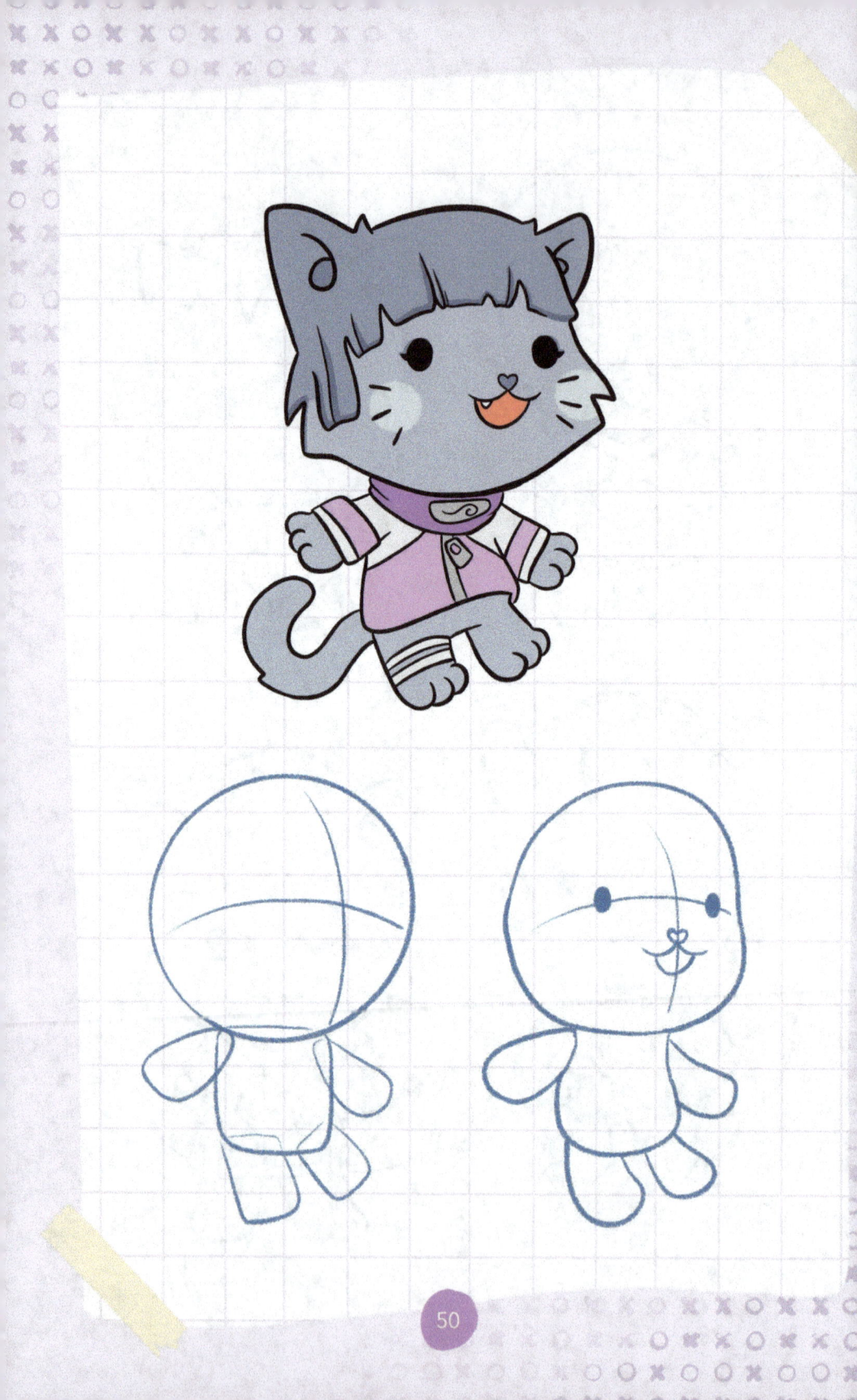

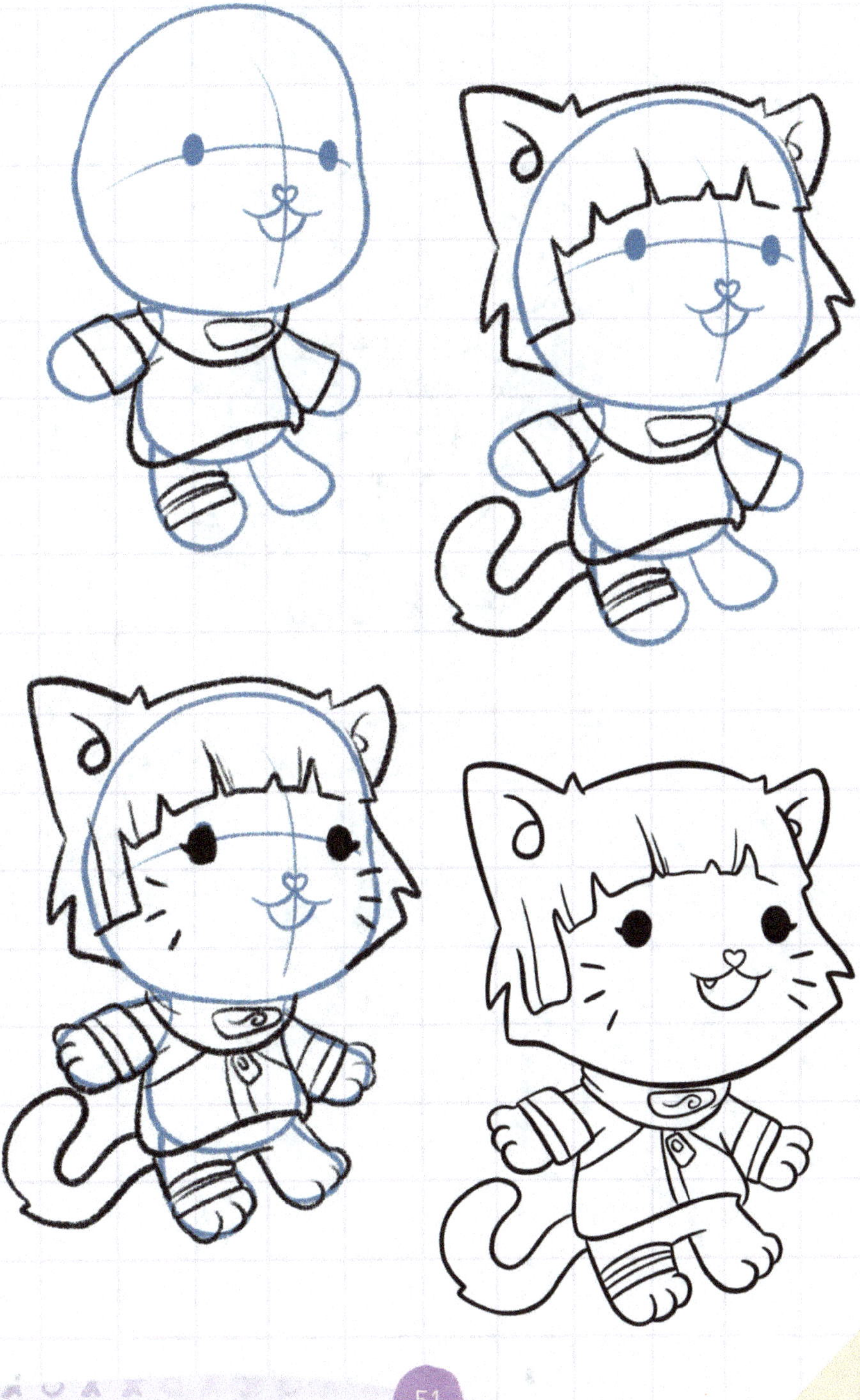

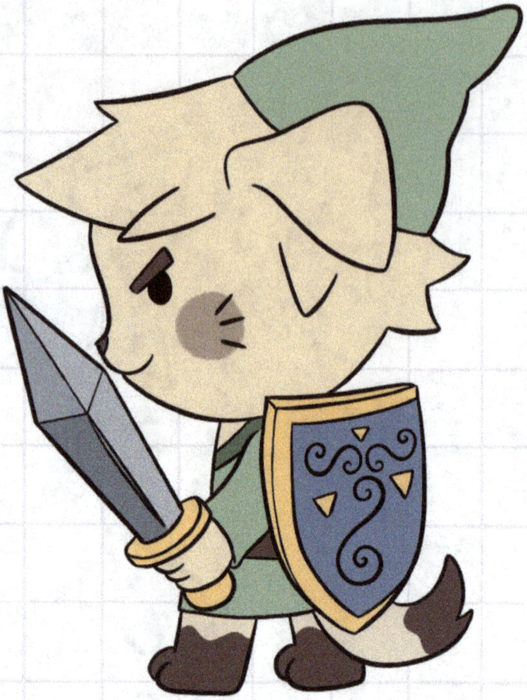

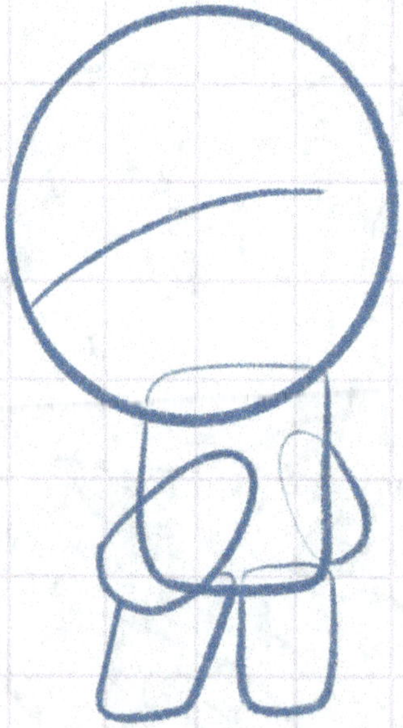

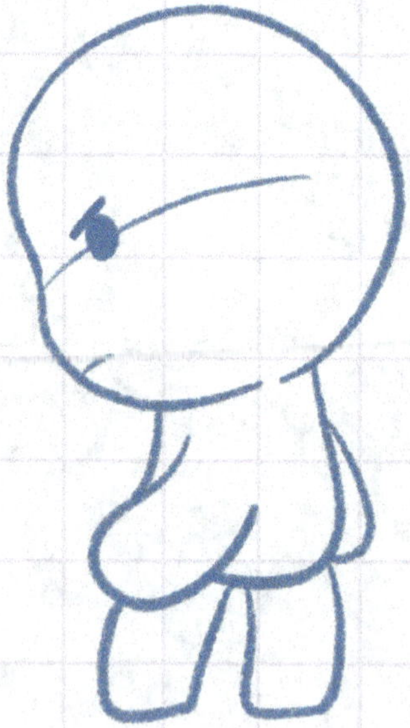

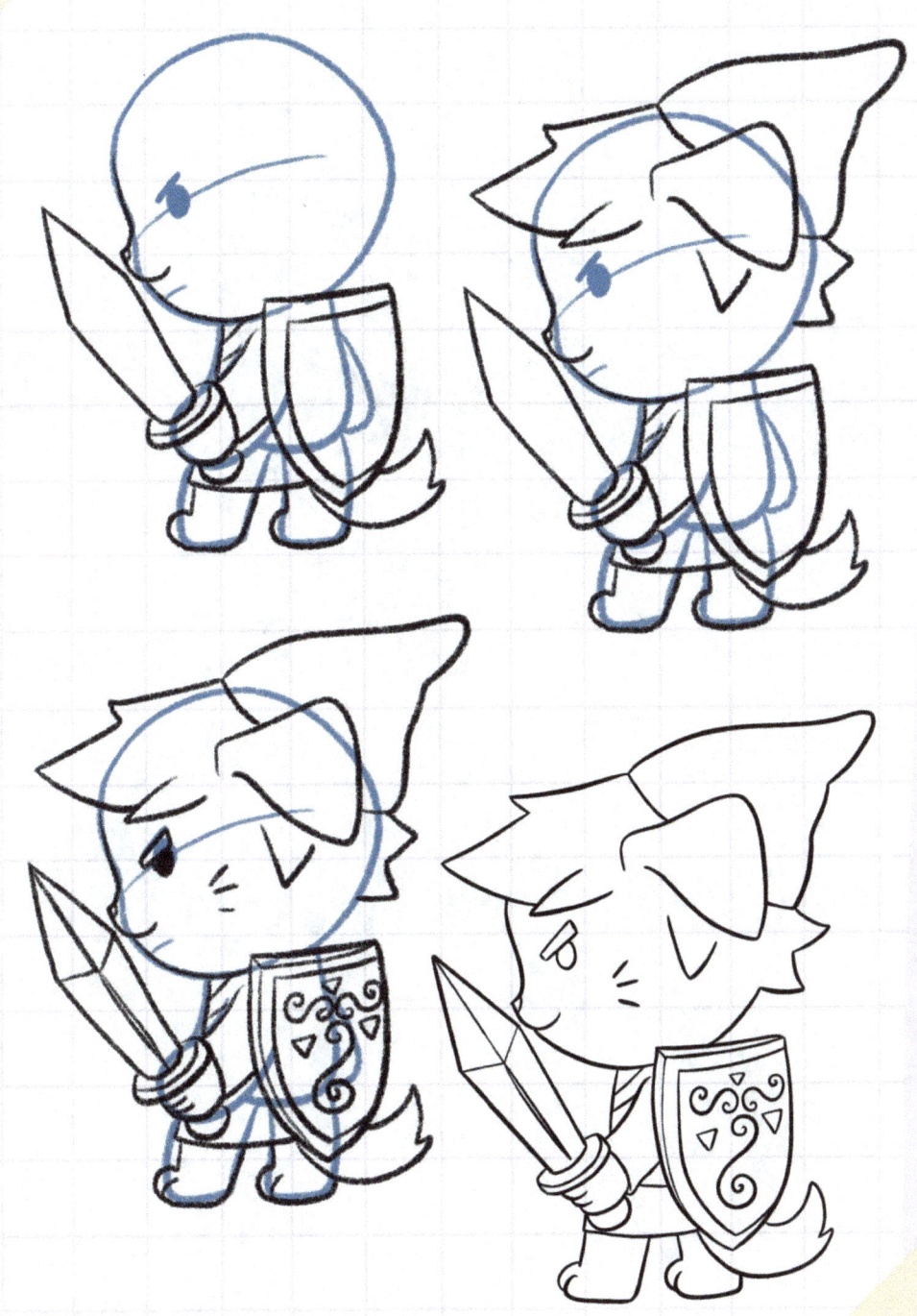

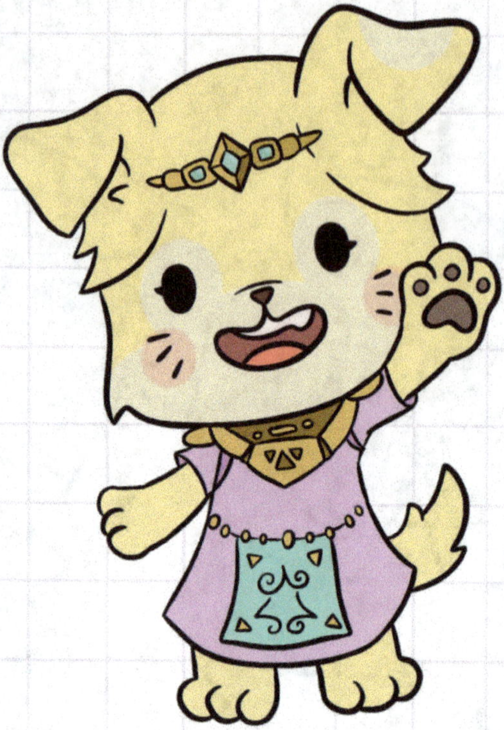

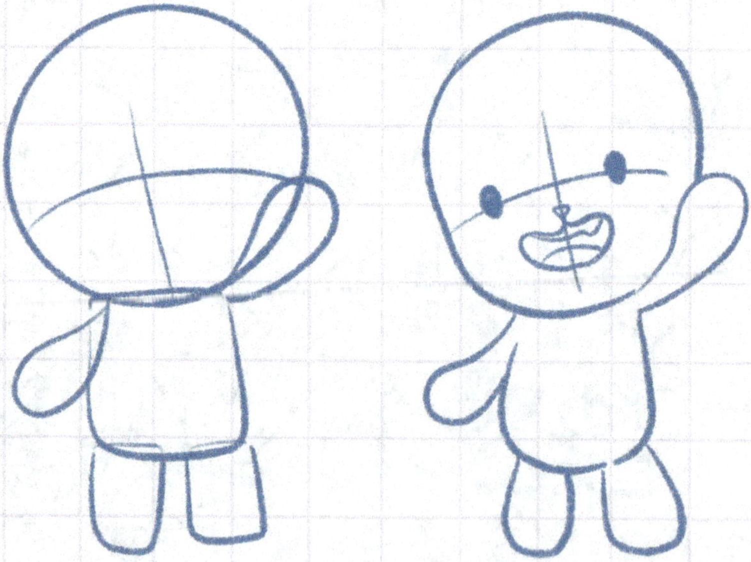

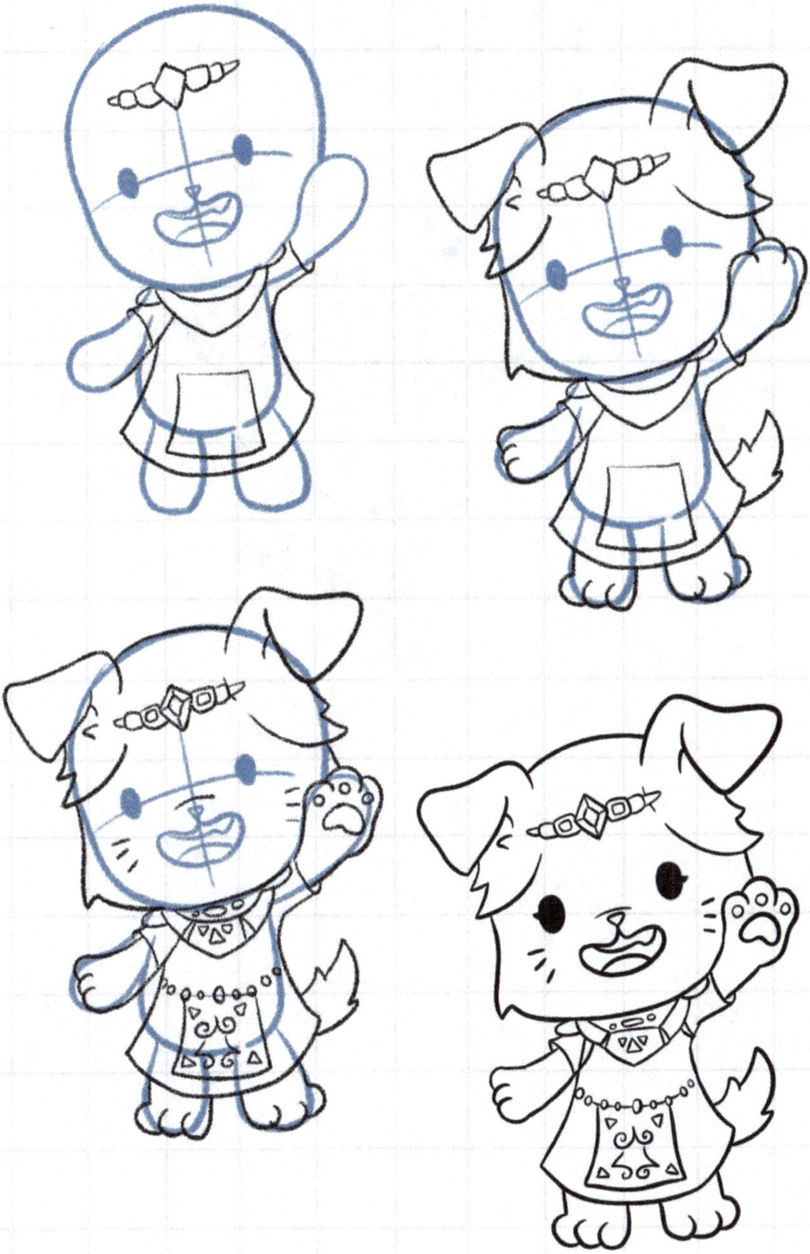

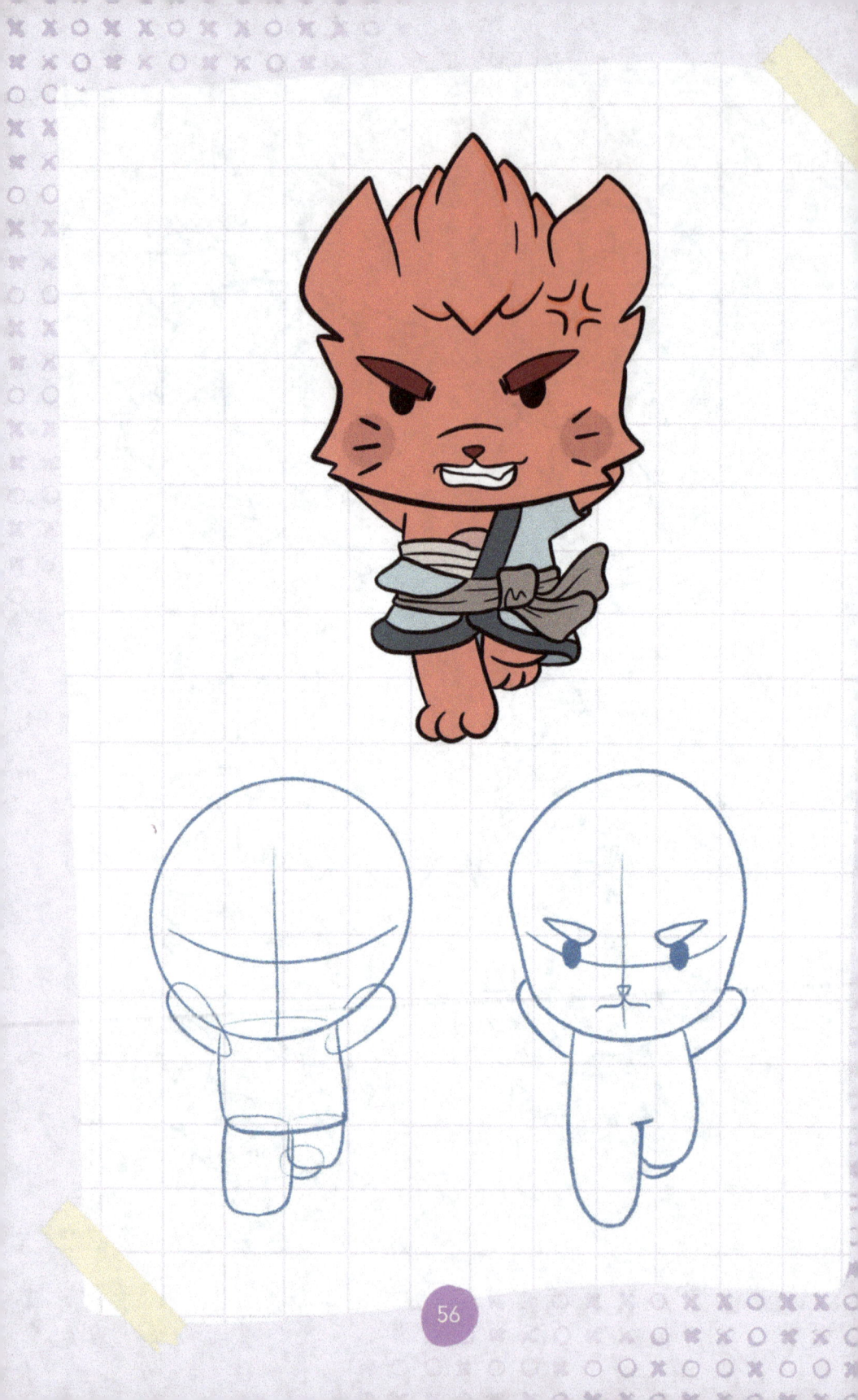

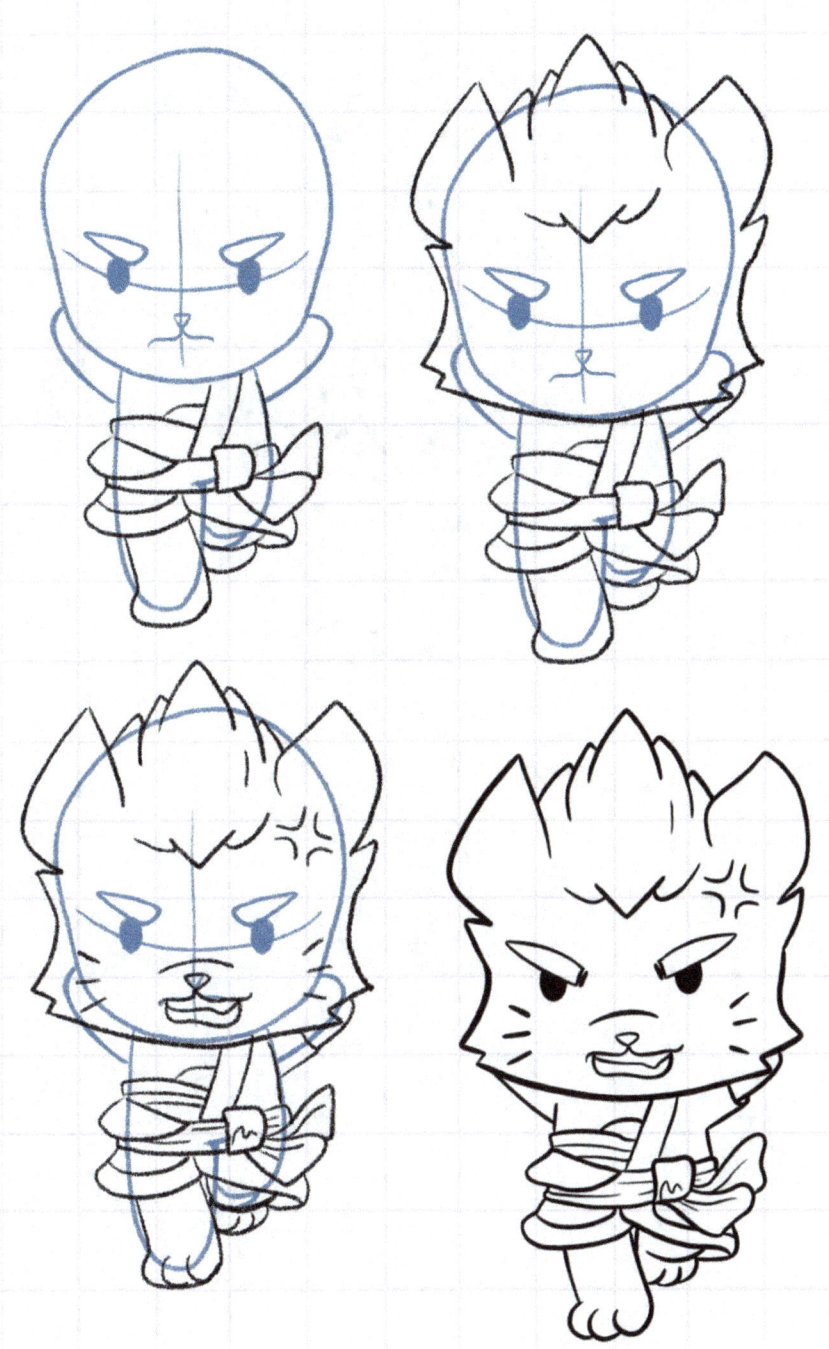

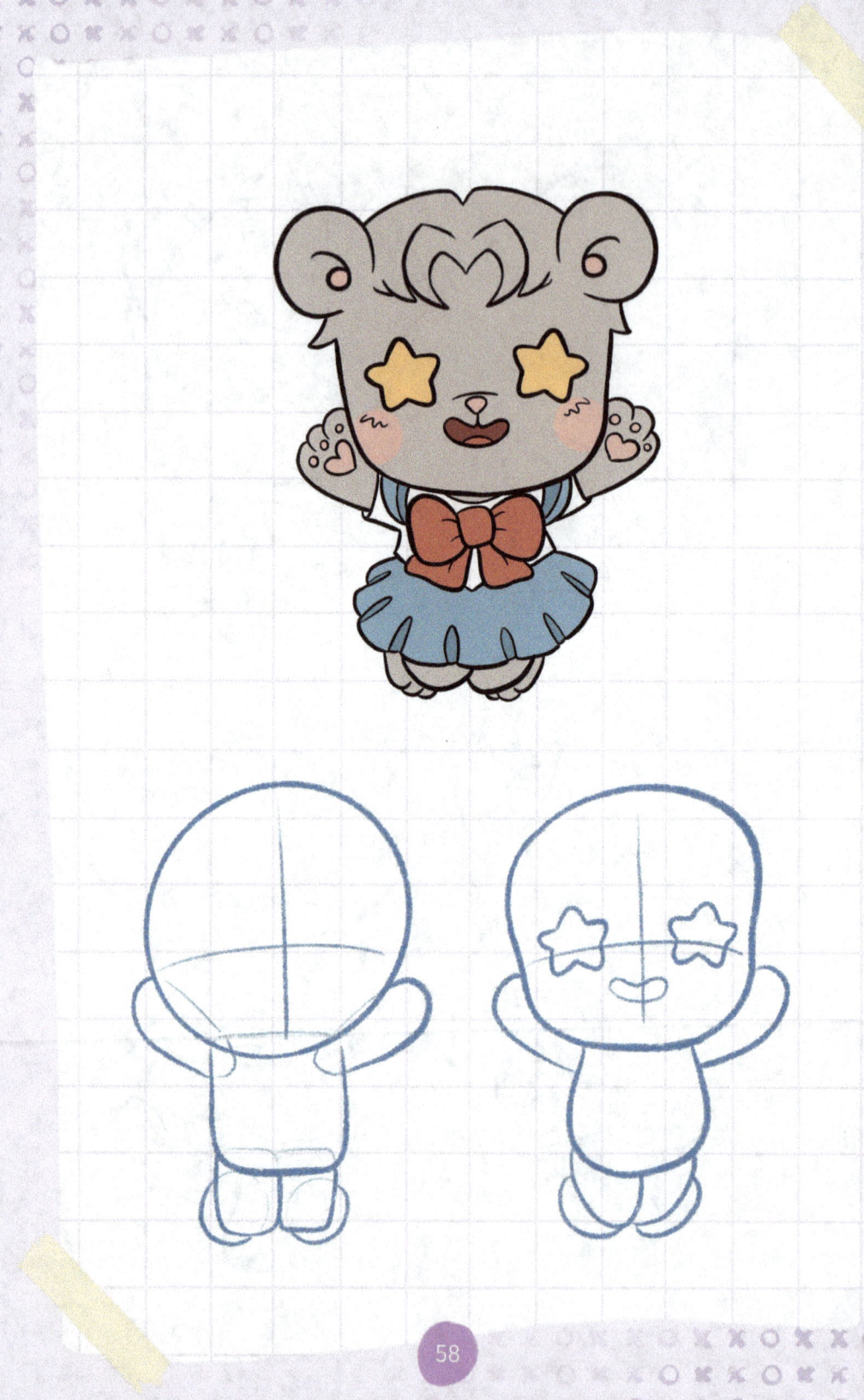

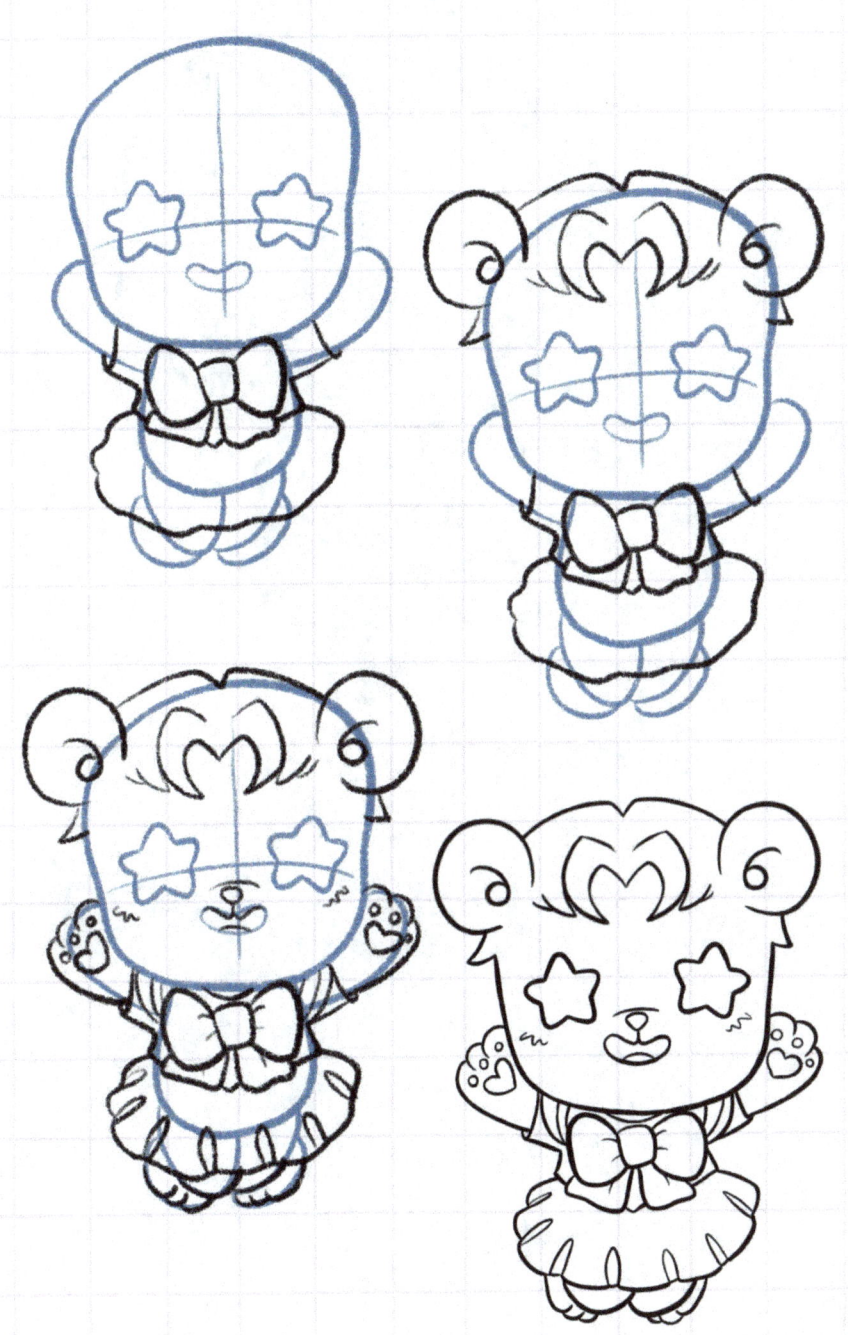

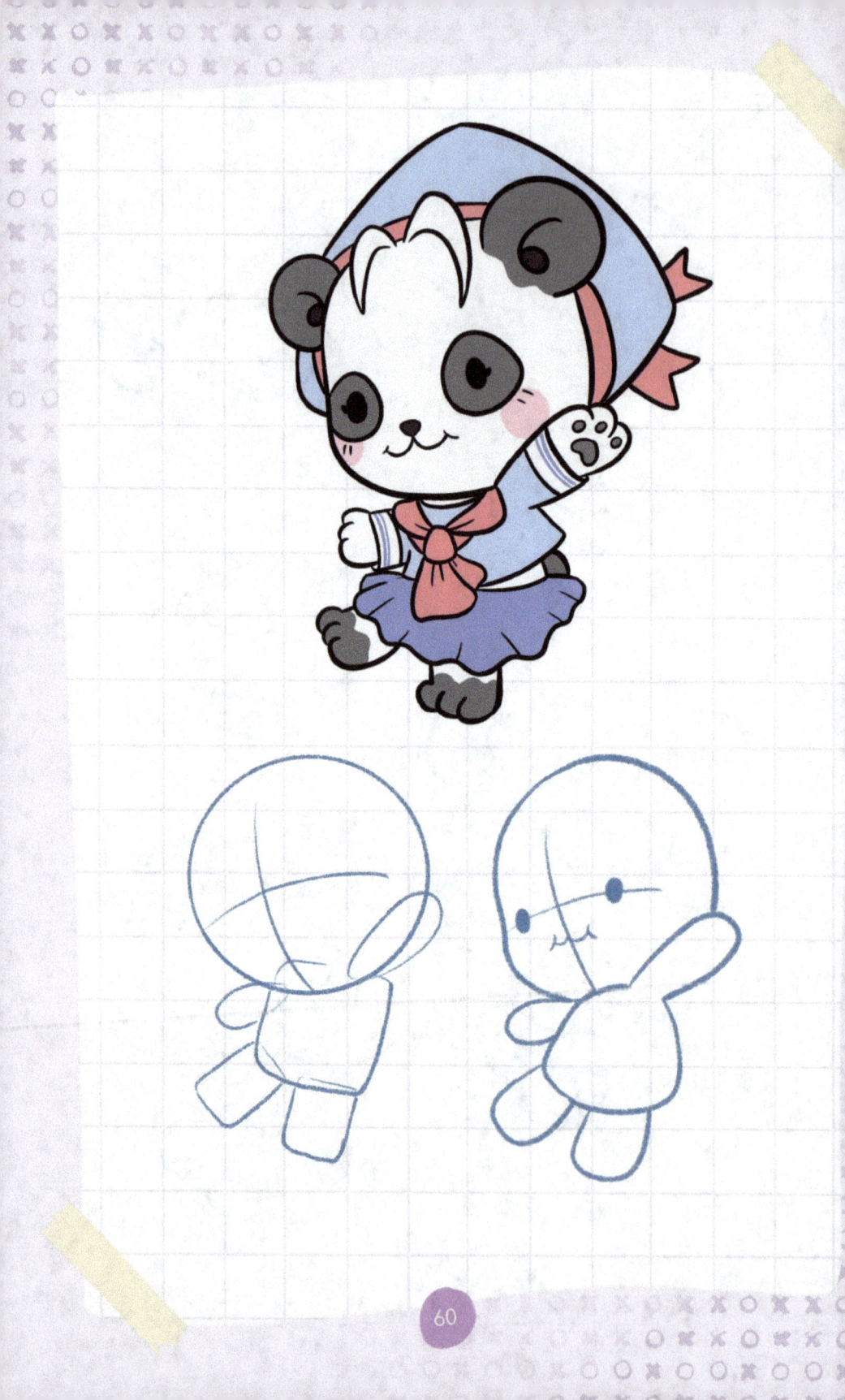

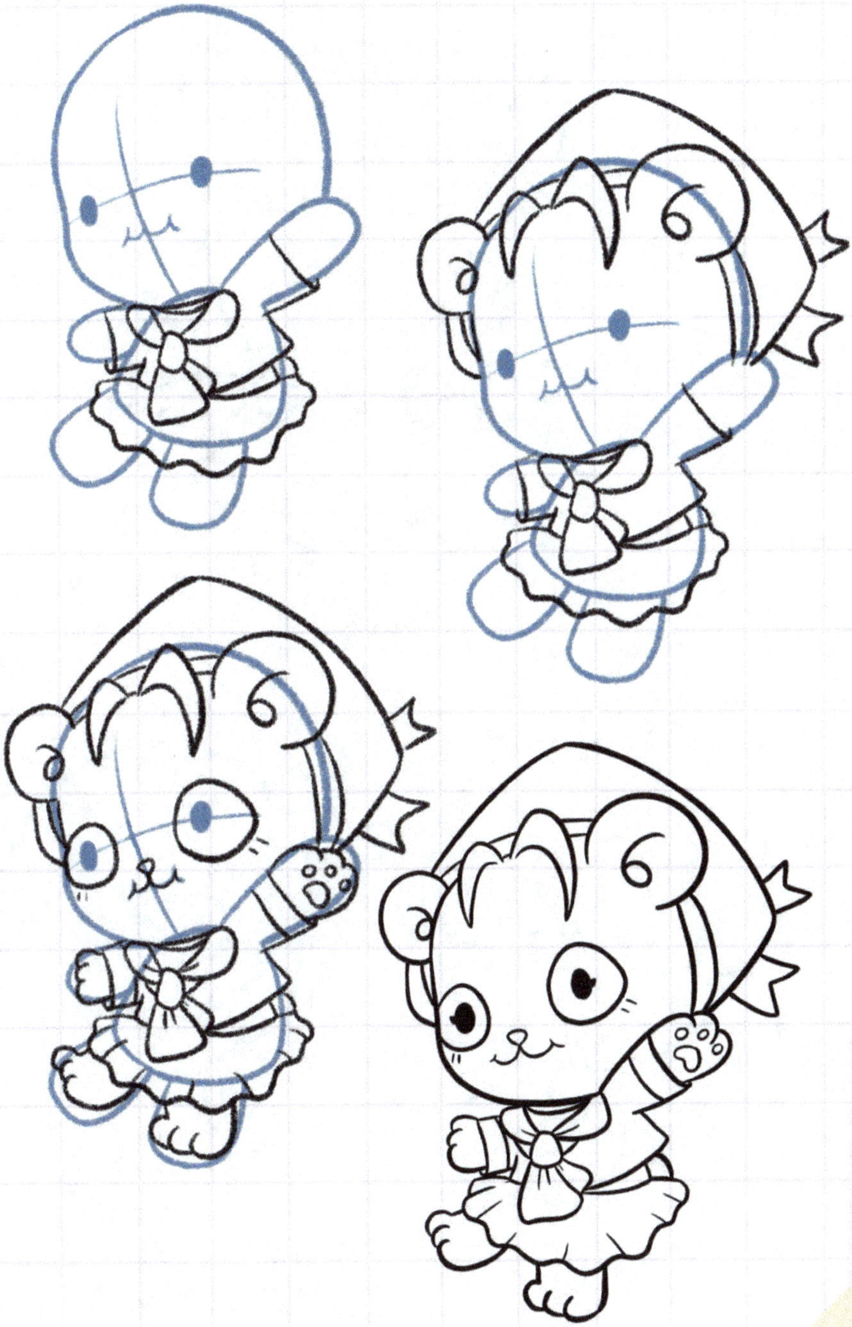

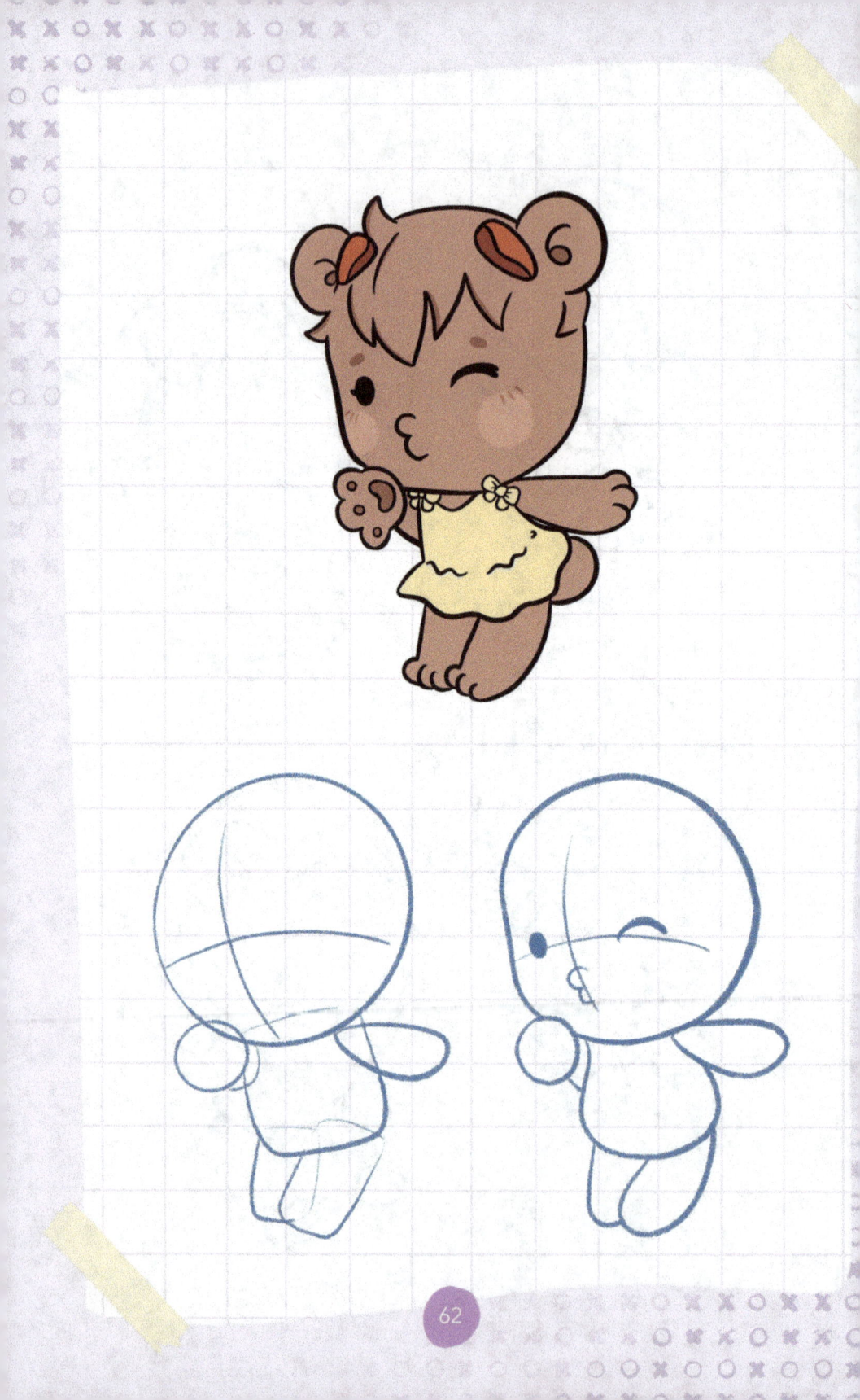

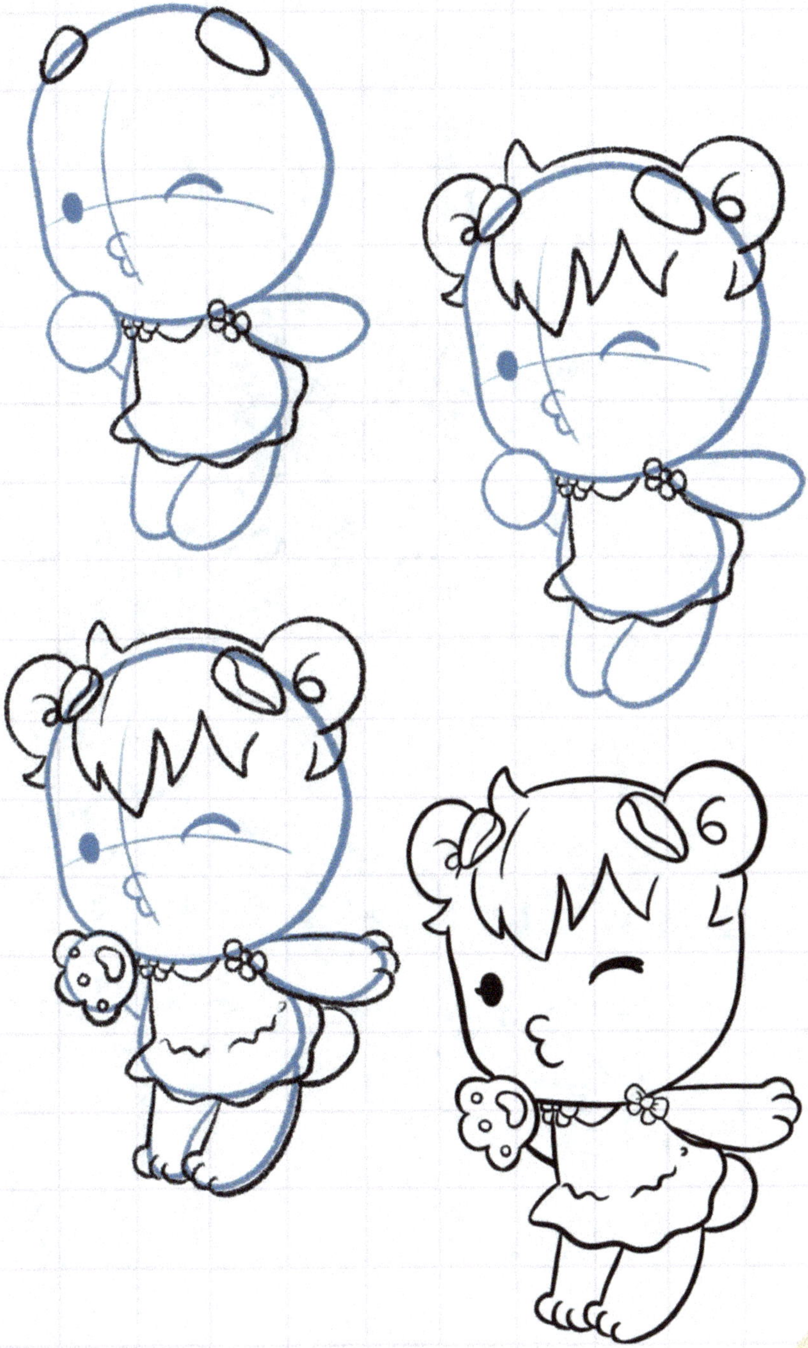

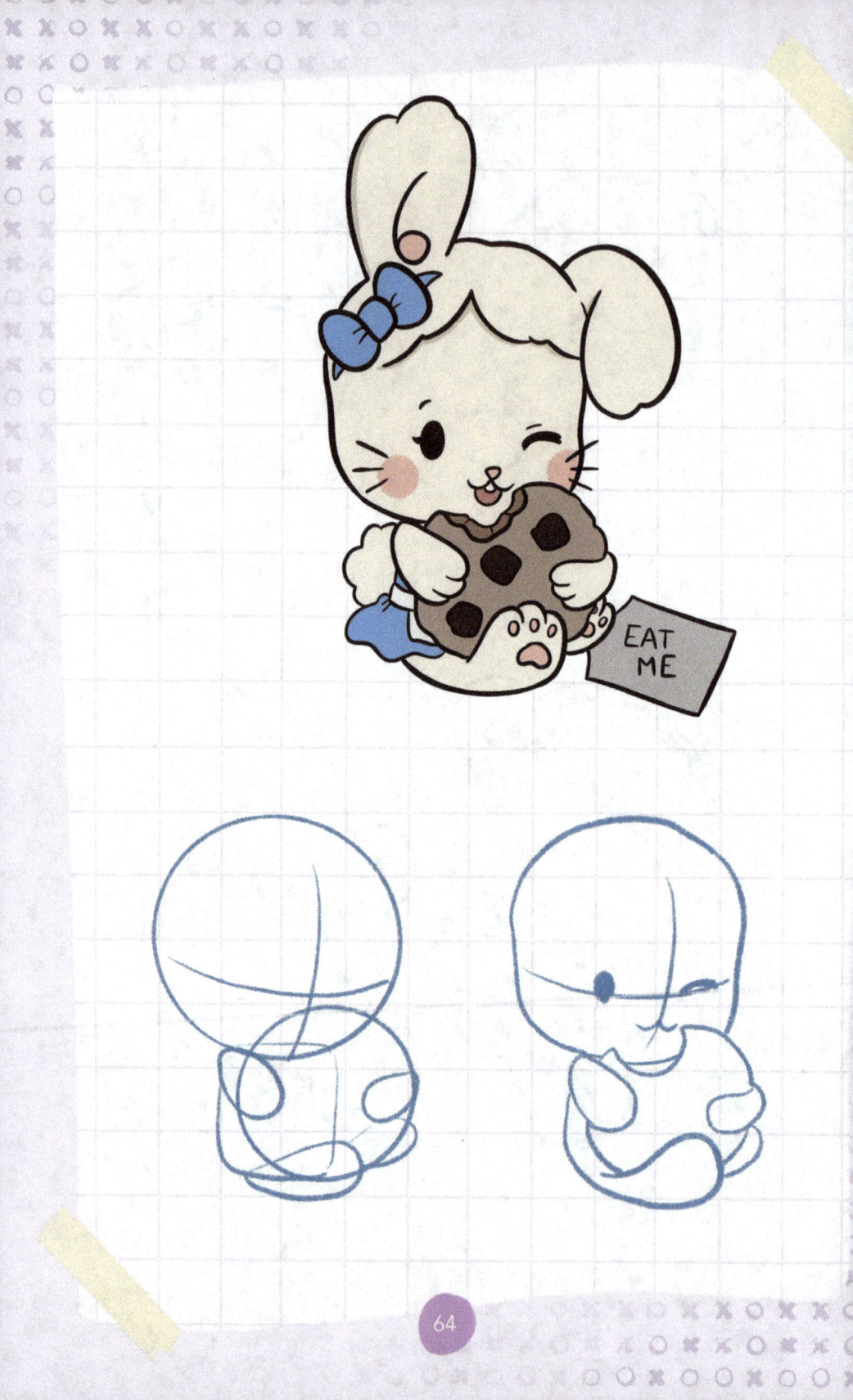

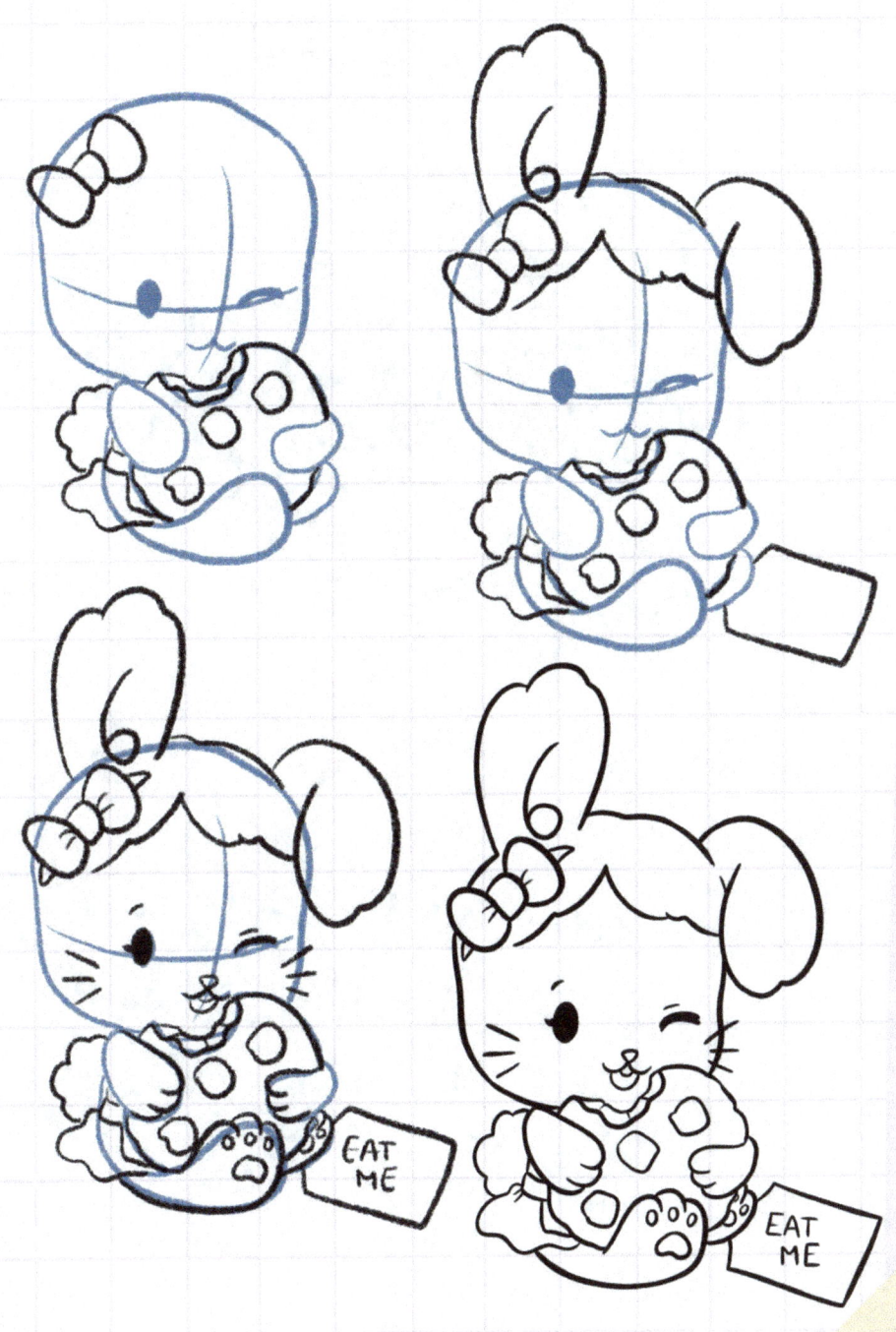

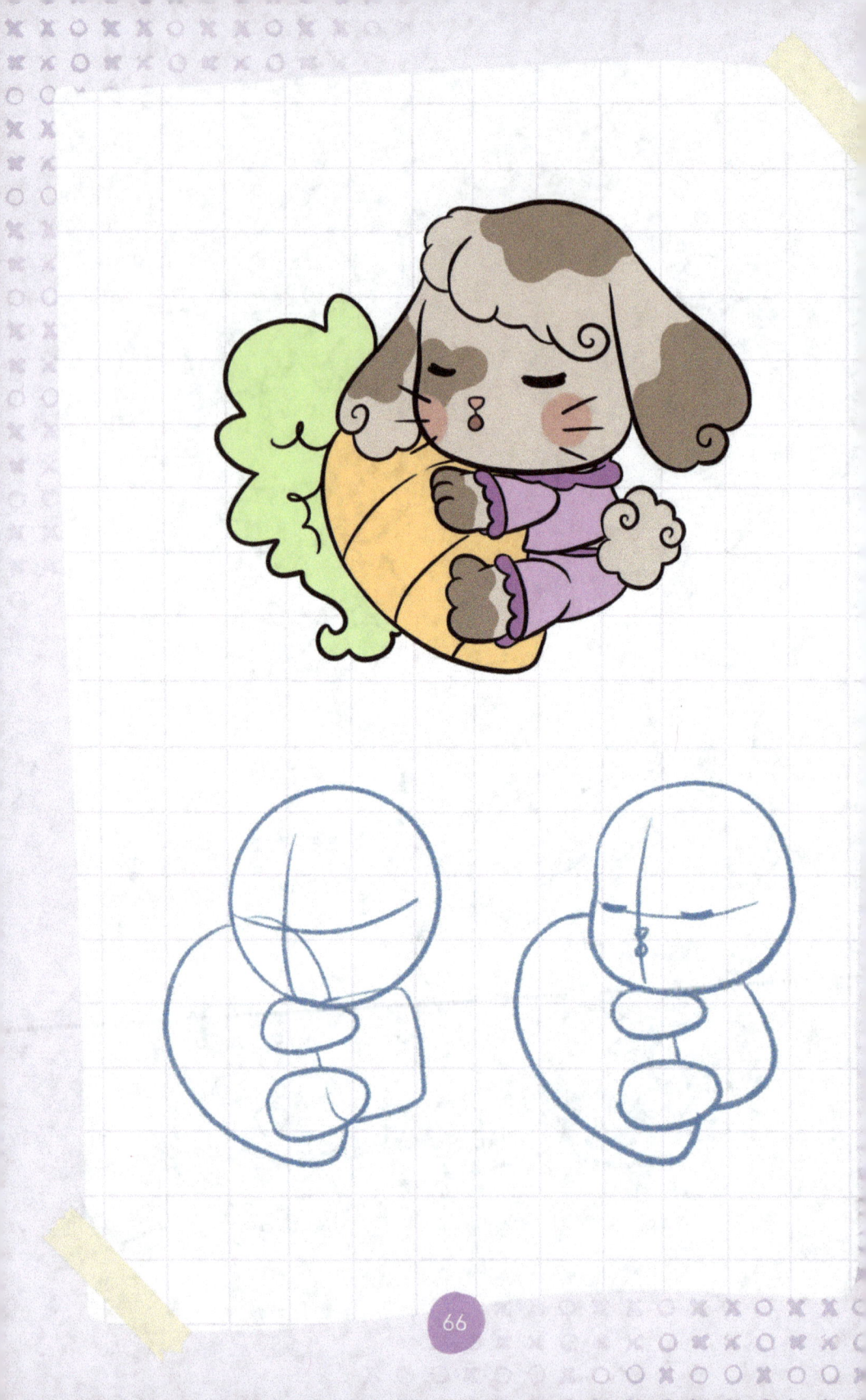

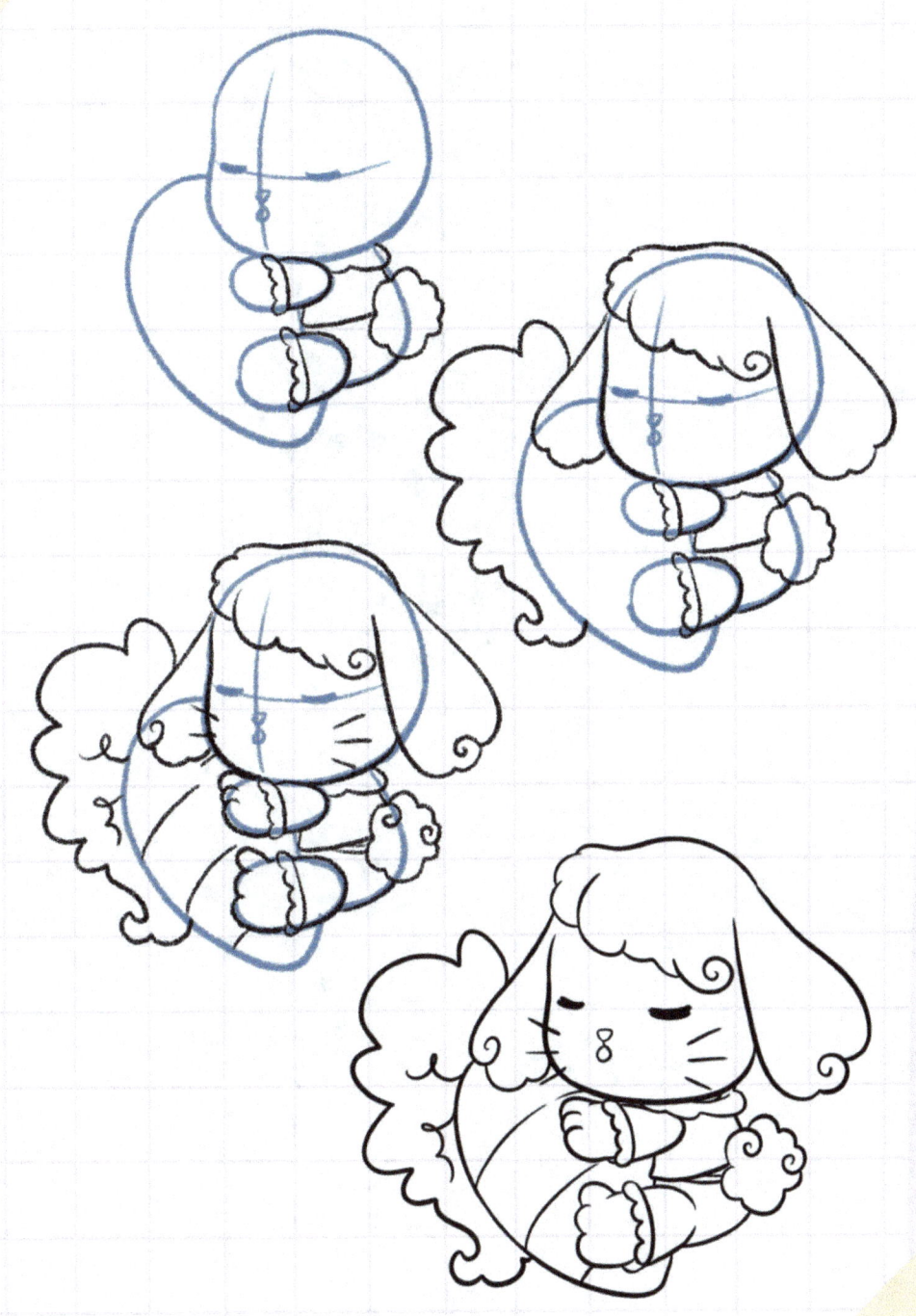

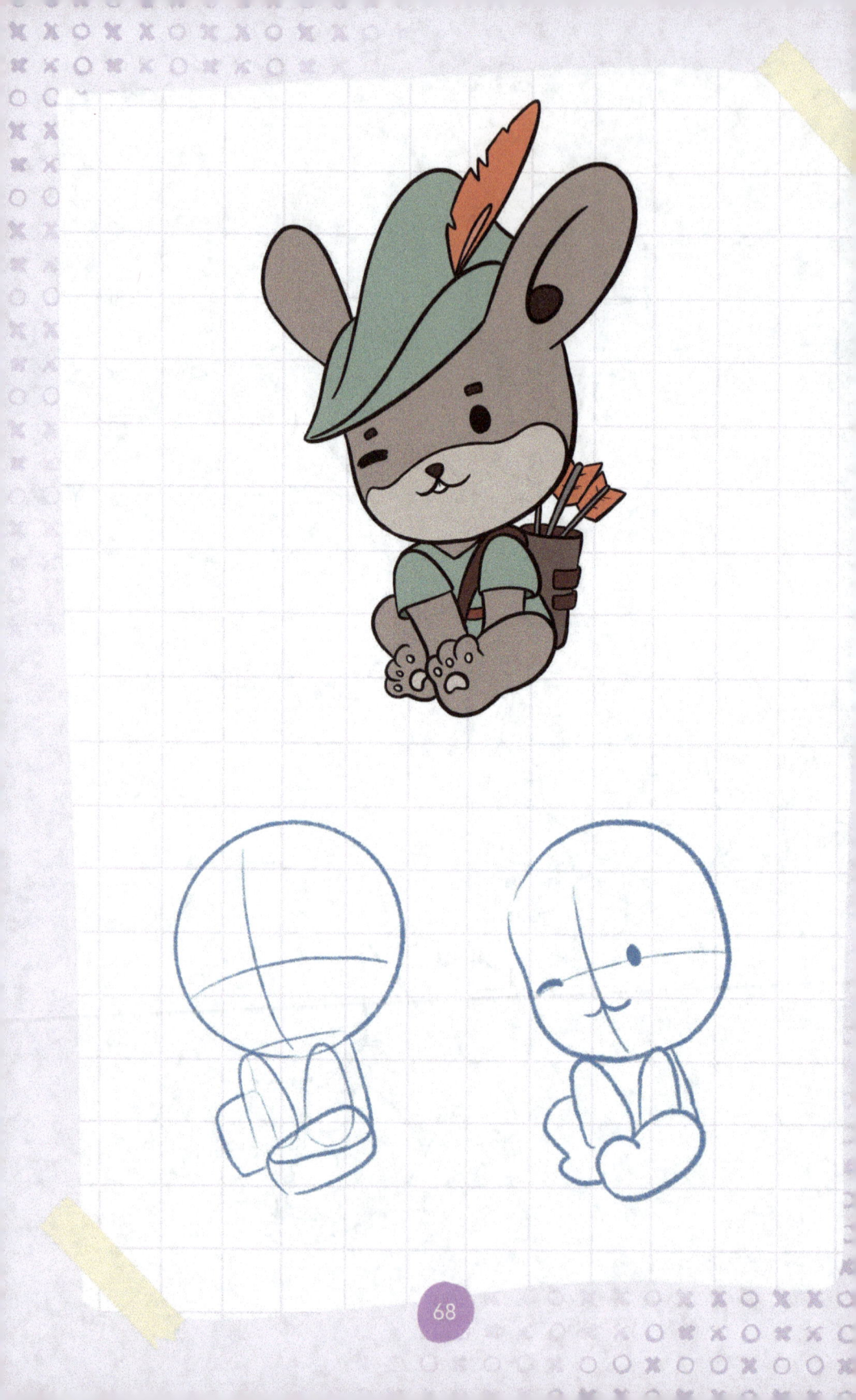

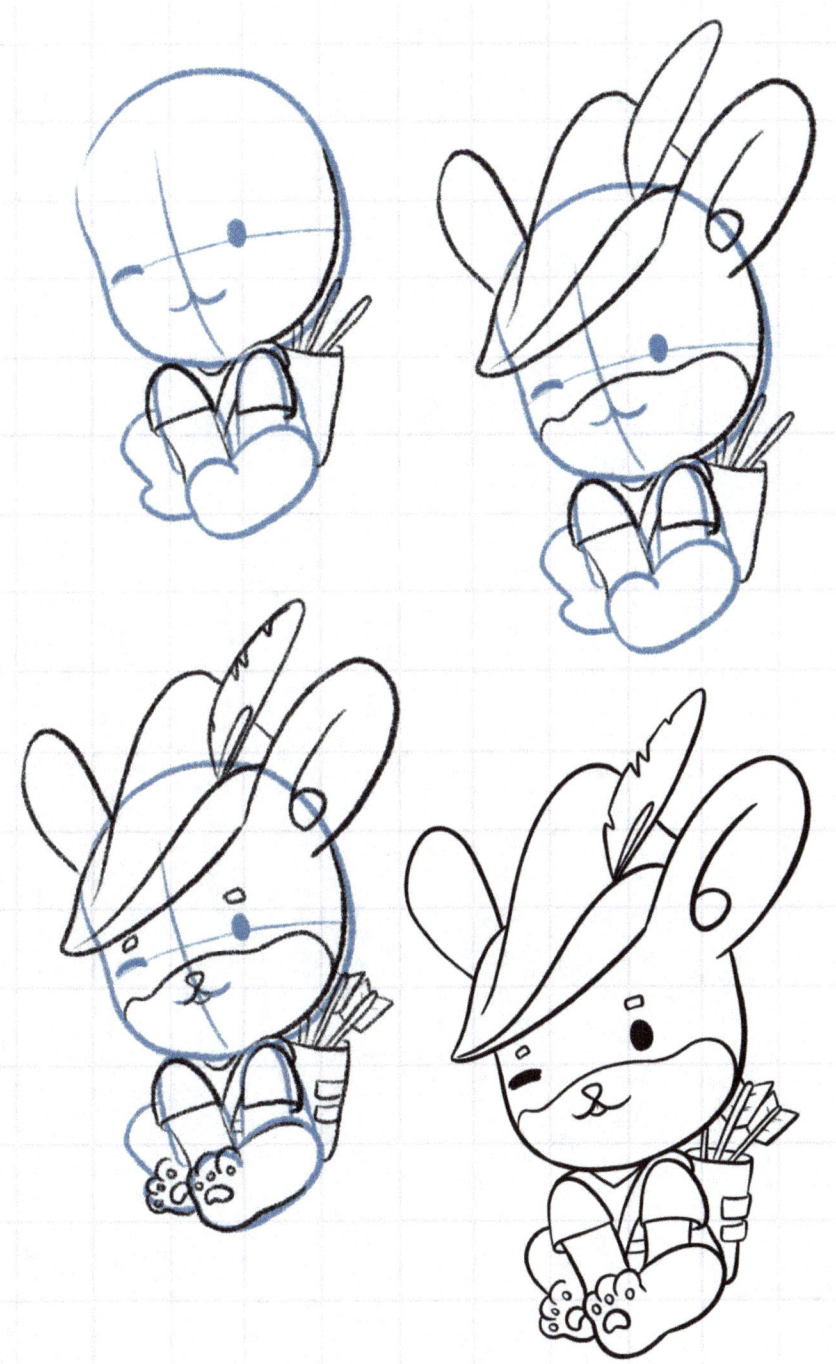

OTHER ANIMALS

THERE ARE DIFFERENT TYPES OF ANIMALS. SO FAR, WE'VE PRACTICED CATS, DOGS, RABBITS, AND BEARS. NOW, WE'RE GOING TO DRAW BIRDS, AMPHIBIANS, AND REPTILES.

THEIR MAIN DIFFERENCES ARE IN THE HANDS, LEGS, AND EVEN THE MOUTH, AS YOU WILL SEE.

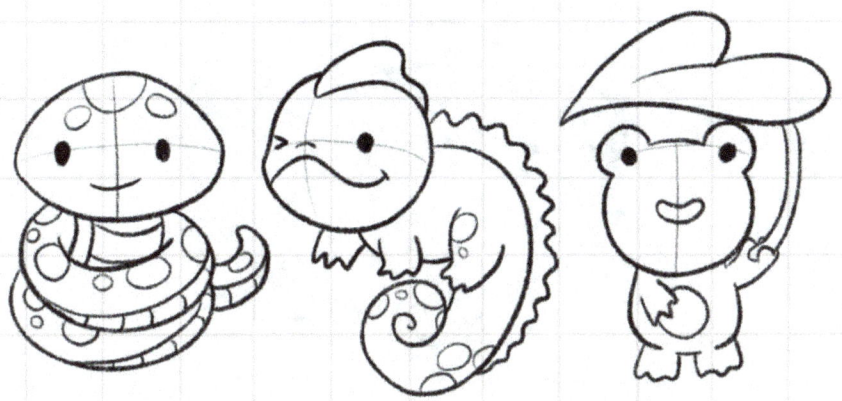

THE SNAKE'S BODY HAS NEITHER LEGS NOR ARMS. THE CHAMELEON HAS AN ELONGATED MOUTH, AND ITS FEET HAVE TRIANGULAR FINGERS, SIMILAR TO THE FROG. THE FROG HAS PROTRUDING EYES DUE TO THE CIRCULAR SHAPE OF ITS HEAD.

BIRDS HAVE BEAKS, AND THEIR HANDS ARE WINGS. THE TOES ON THEIR FEET END IN TRIANGULAR SHAPES.

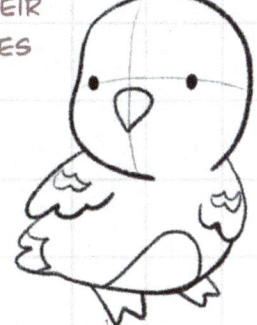

LET'S PRACTICE STEP BY STEP WITH THESE FIGURES.

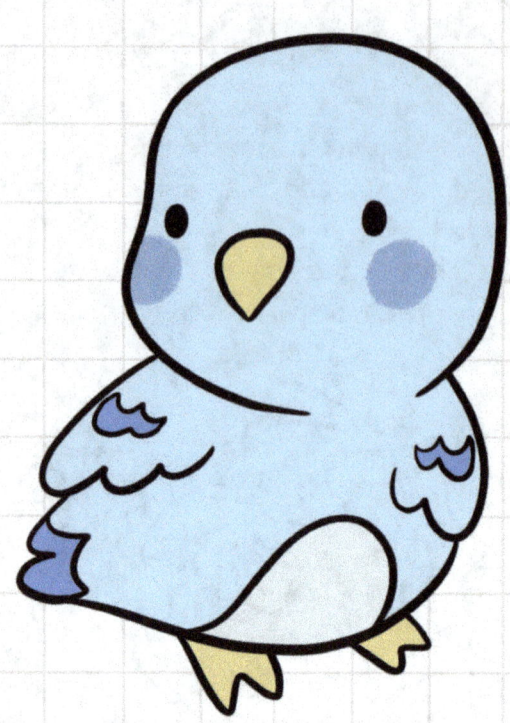

START BY SKETCHING WITH SIMPLE SHAPES, A CIRCLE FOR THE
HEAD AND A SMALLER ONE FOR THE BODY. AND TWO SMALLER
CIRCLES THAT WILL BE ITS WINGS.

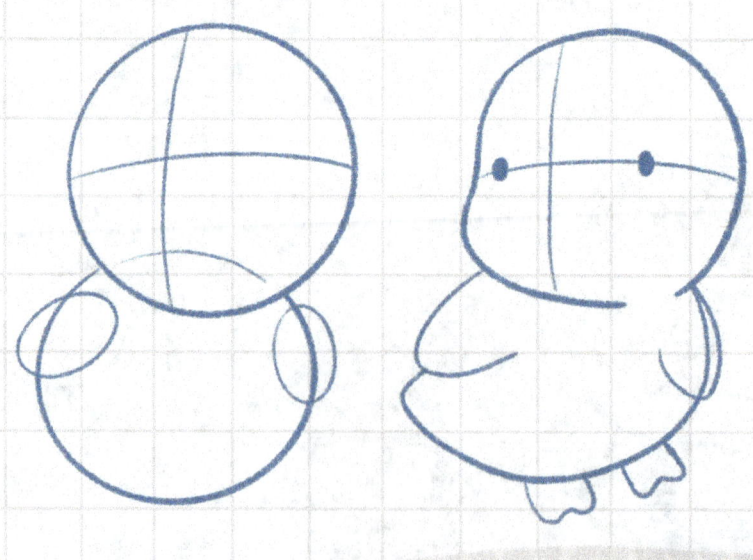

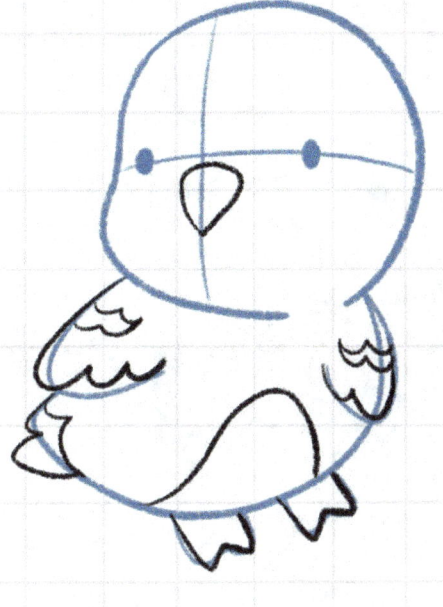

THE EYES WILL BE PLACED ON THE GUIDE CROSS, BUT IN THIS CASE, INSTEAD OF A MOUTH, IT HAS A BEAK.

LET'S ROUND THE FEATHERS ON ITS WINGS AND TAIL.

ITS LEGS END IN TRIANGULAR TOES.

FINALLY, GO OVER IT WITH A MARKER AND ERASE THE PENCIL TO COLOR IT HOWEVER YOU LIKE.

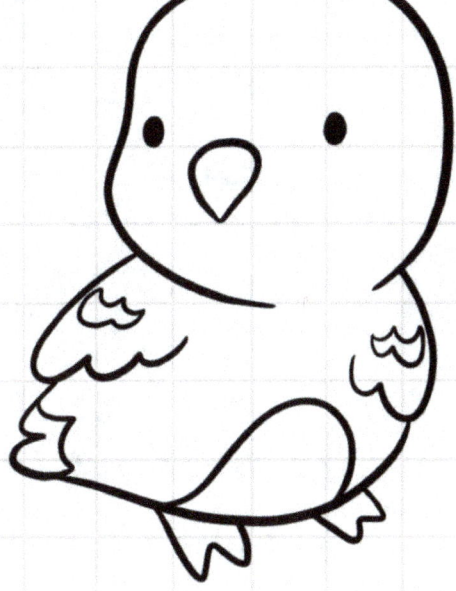

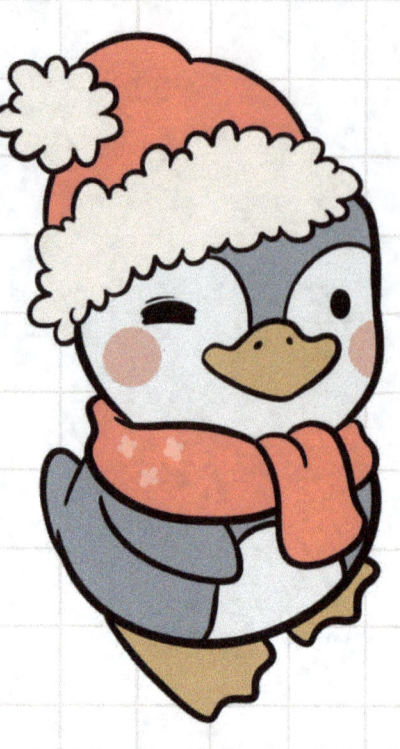

NOW, LET'S DRAW A PENGUIN. AS YOU CAN SEE, ITS
BEAK IS LONGER, AND ITS FEET HAVE THREE
TRIANGULAR TOES.

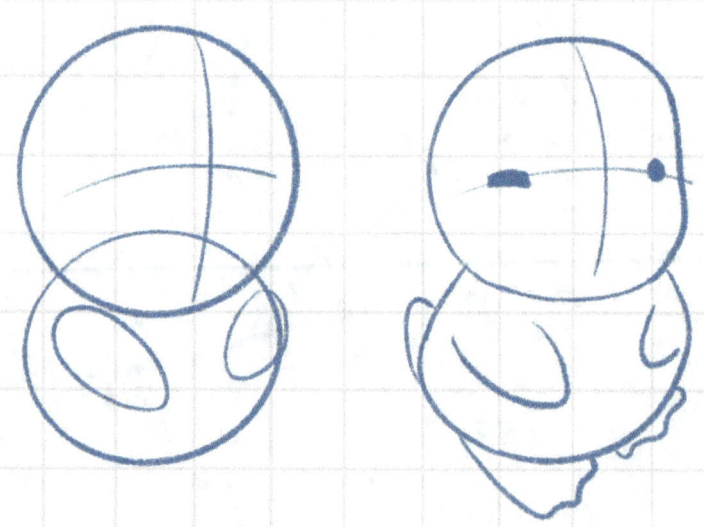

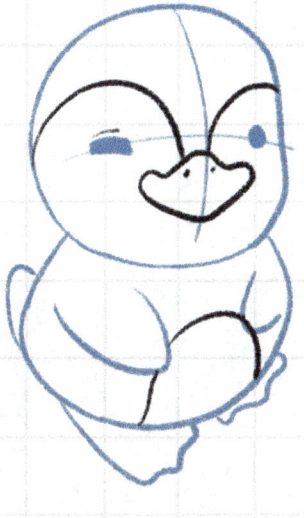

THE PENGUIN CAN'T FLY, SO LET'S MAKE ITS WINGS WITHOUT FEATHERS.

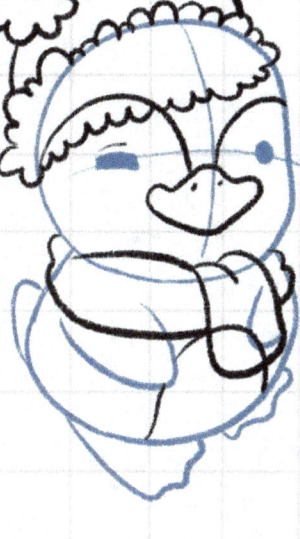

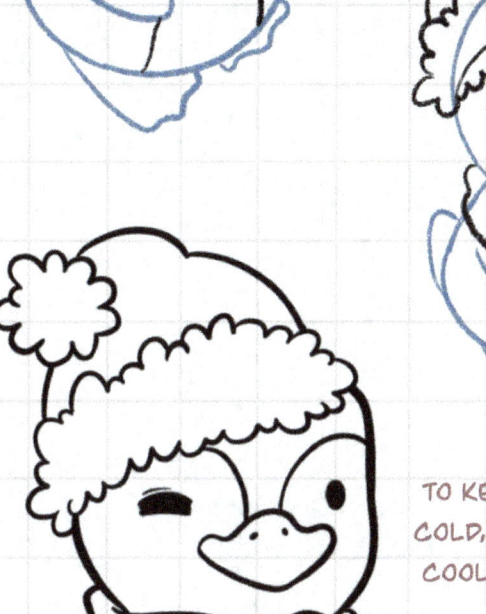

TO KEEP IT FROM GETTING COLD, LET'S DRAW A SUPER COOL HAT AND SCARF FOR IT.

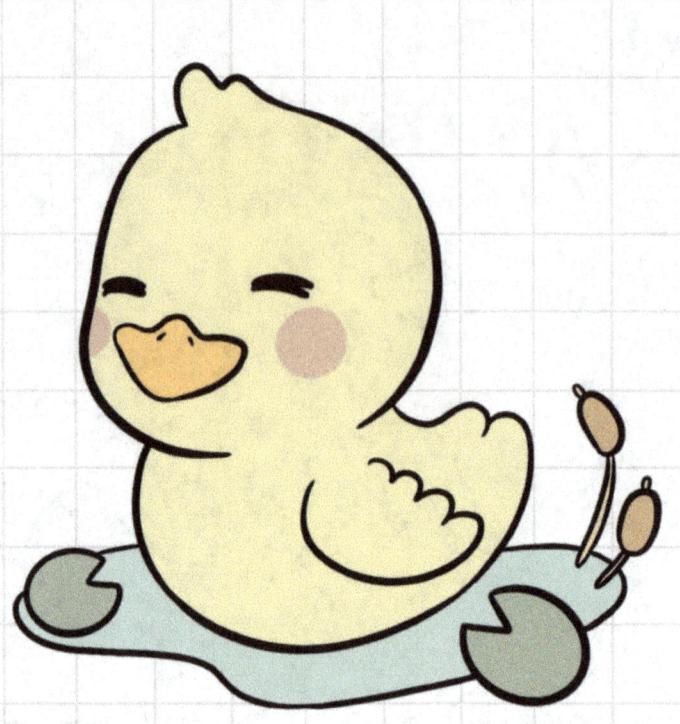

THIS DUCK HIDES ITS LEGS IN THE WATER WHILE SWIMMING.

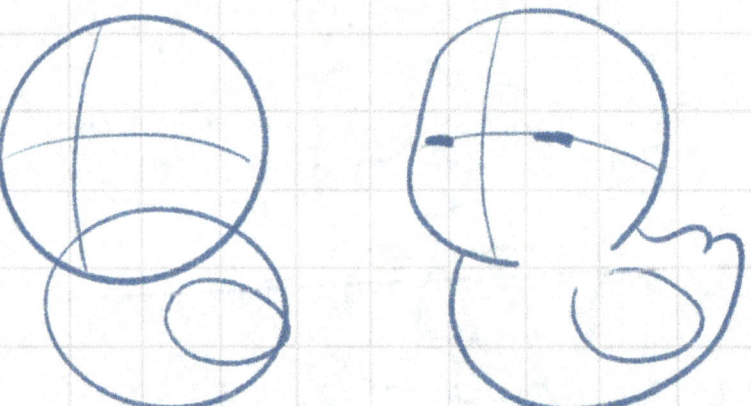

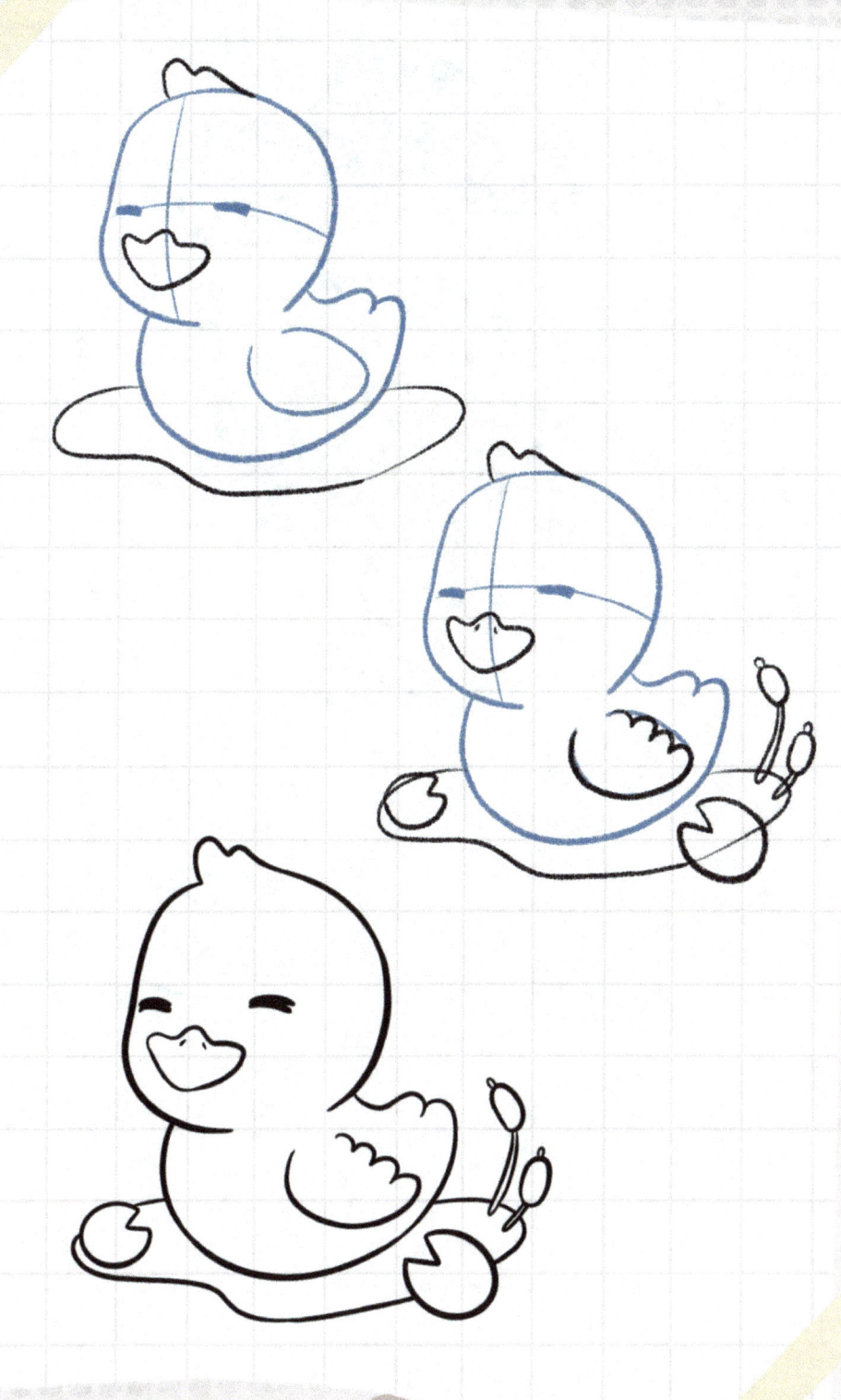

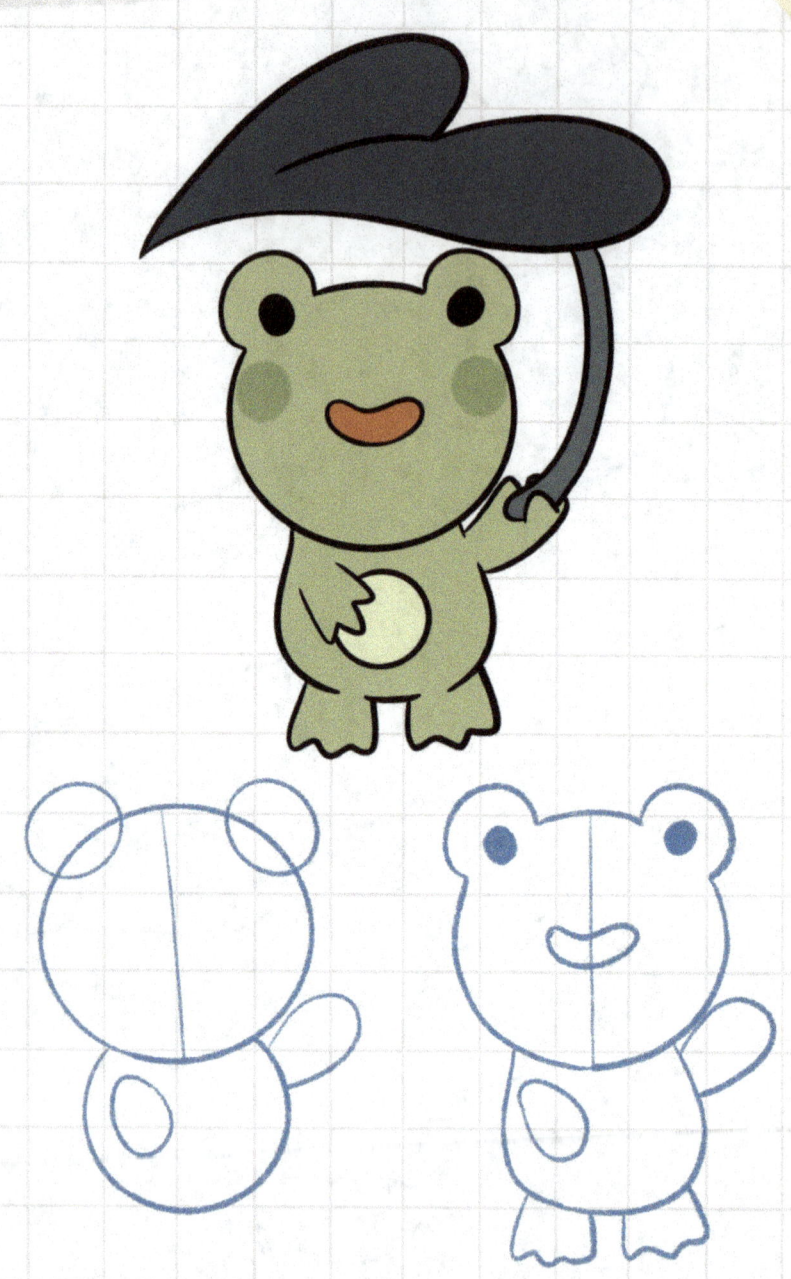

TO SKETCH THE FROG, WE'RE GOING TO USE A CIRCLE FOR
ITS HEAD WITH TWO SMALLER CIRCLES FOR ITS EYES, AND A
SMALLER CIRCLE FOR THE BODY.

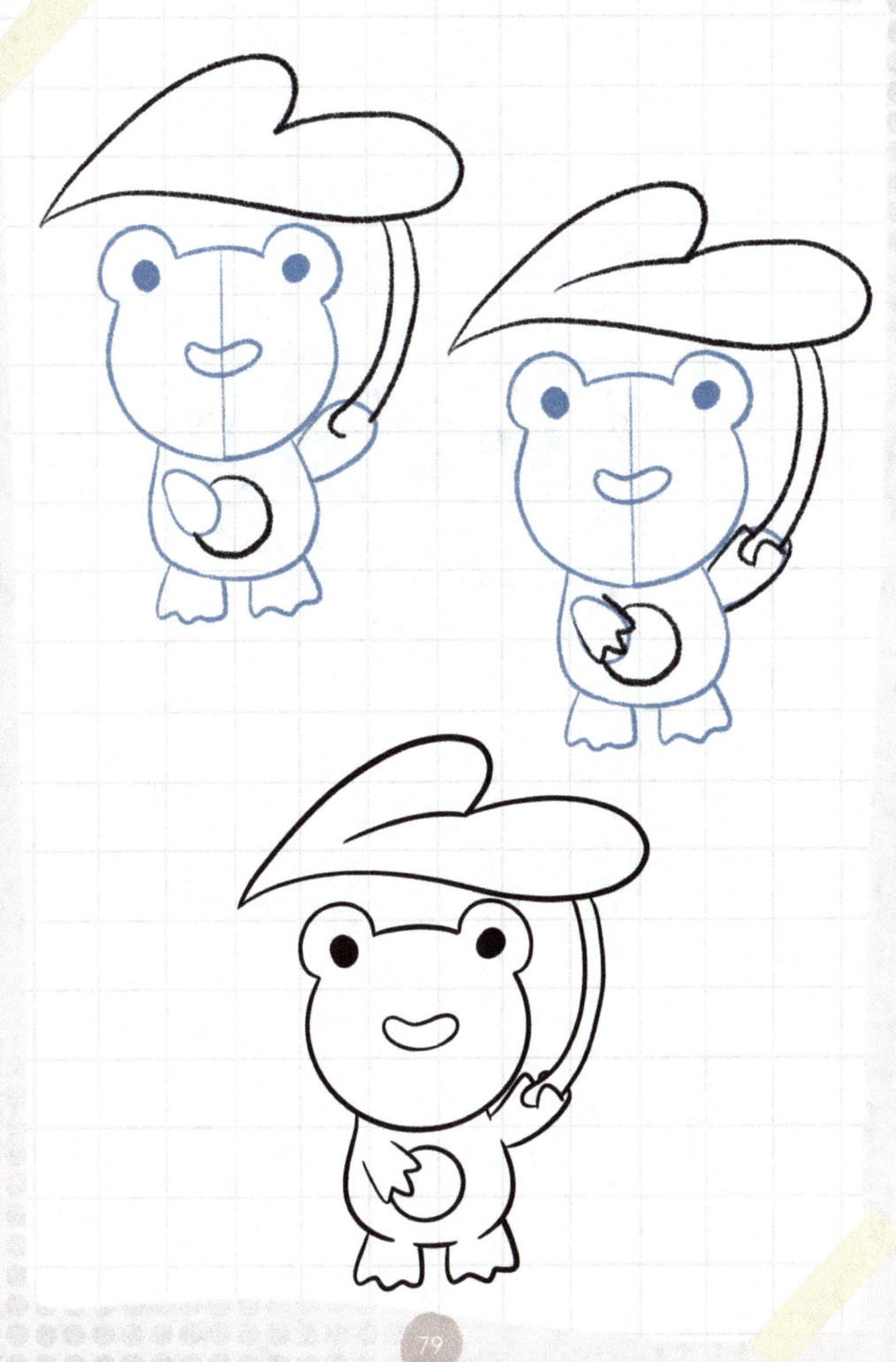

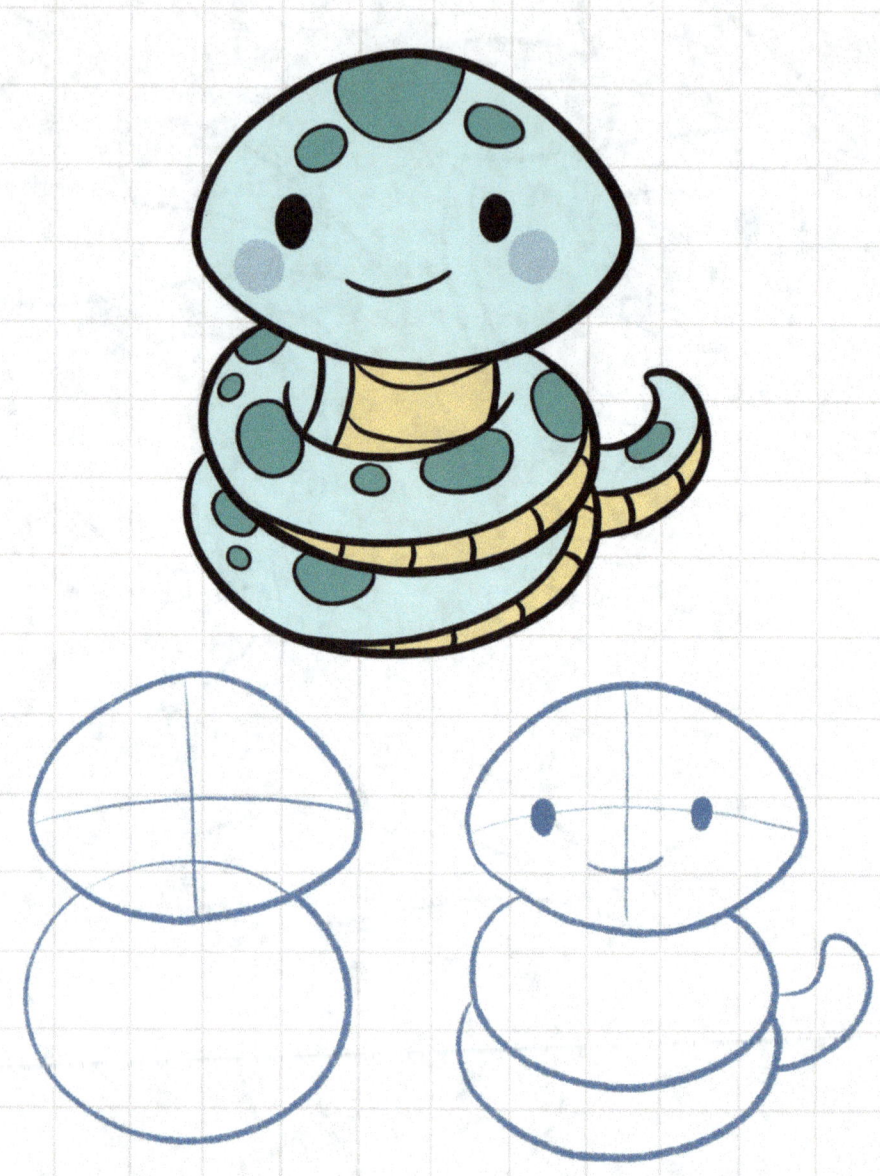

THE SNAKE MAY SEEM SIMPLER, BUT IT CAN ACTUALLY BE MORE CHALLENGING. START BY SKETCHING WITH TWO CIRCLES OF SIMILAR SIZE FOR THE HEAD AND BODY. NOW, DIVIDE THE LOWER CIRCLE WITH A SEMICIRCLE.

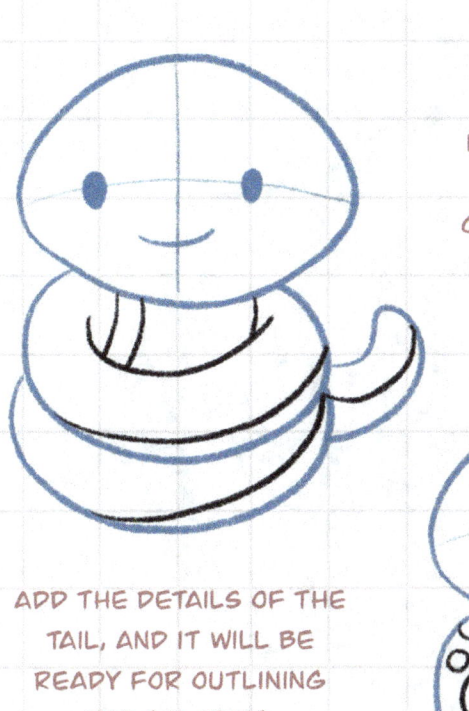

PAY ATTENTION TO THE INTERNAL DETAILS. DRAW THE NECK, AND COMPLETE THE SHAPE OF THE FIGURE WITH SEMICIRCLES.

ADD THE DETAILS OF THE TAIL, AND IT WILL BE READY FOR OUTLINING AND COLORING.

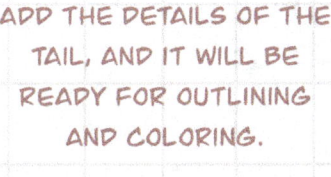

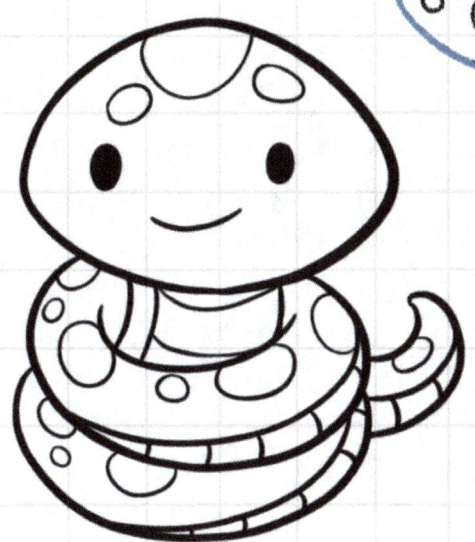

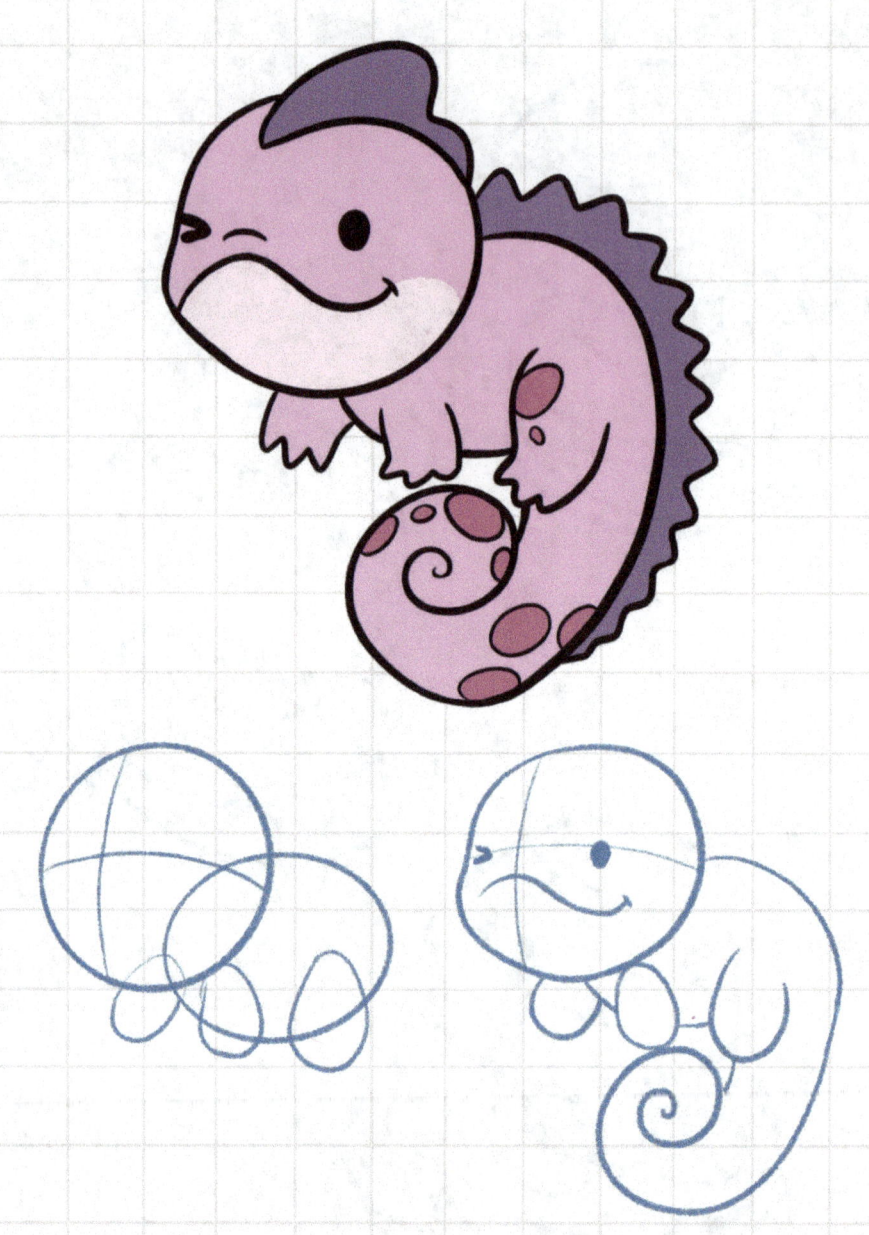

THE CHAMELEON IS A LOT OF FUN, IT HAS A MUCH LONGER MOUTH AND A TAIL THAT IS ALMOST AS LARGE AS THE REST OF ITS BODY.

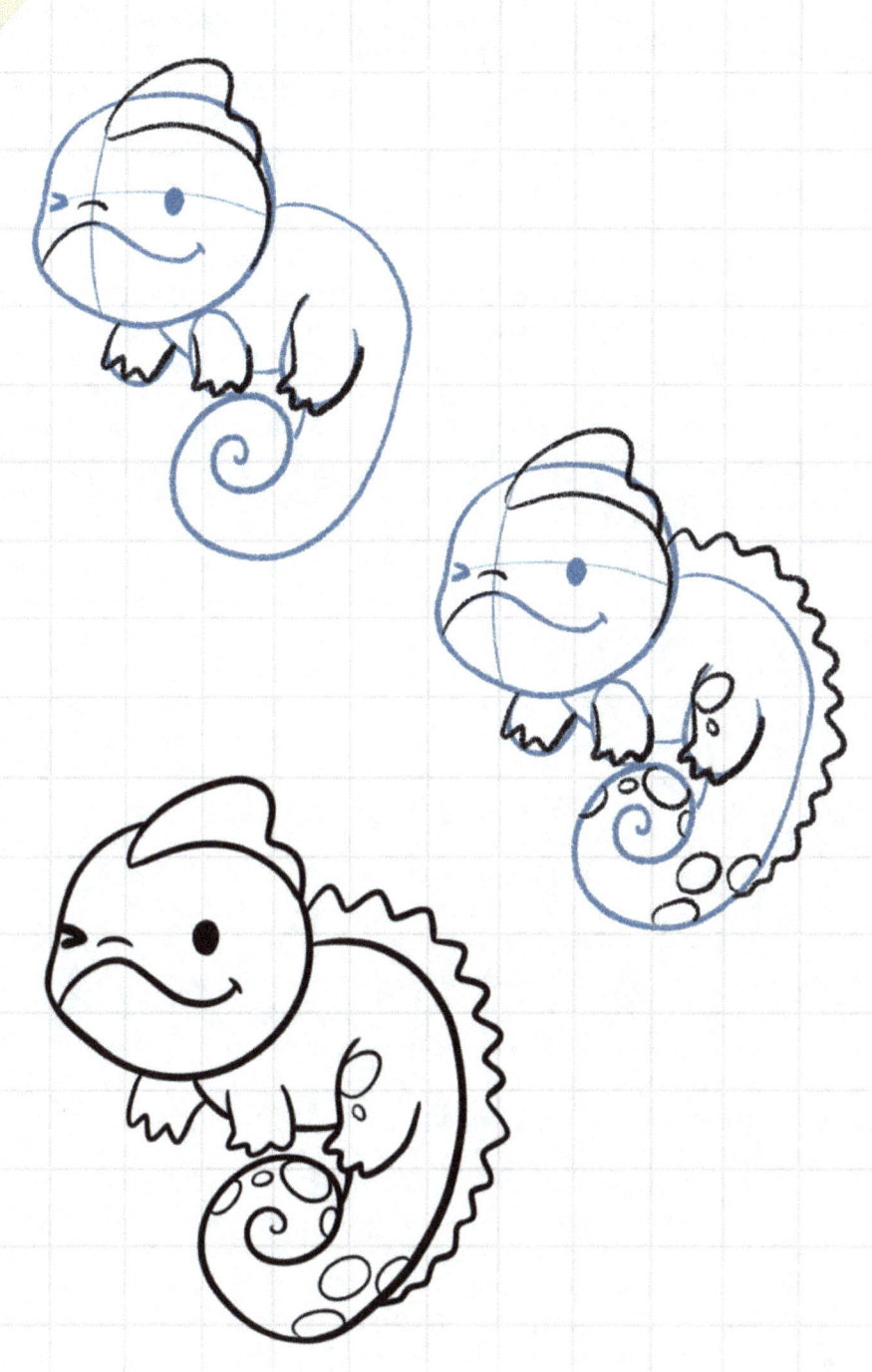

KAWAII FOOD

CREATING KAWAII FOOD IS A LOT OF FUN. LET'S PRACTICE WITH DIFFERENT FOODS, SWEETS, AND DISHES.

YOU CAN CONTINUE DRAWING KAWAII FOOD OF ANY FAVORITE FOOD, FRUIT, OR DISH BY ADDING THE KAWAII EXPRESSIONS WE'VE PRACTICED THROUGHOUT THE COURSE.

REMEMBER TO START THE SKETCH WITH SIMPLE SHAPES LIKE CIRCLES, SQUARES, AND TRIANGLES. ROUND AND REFINE THEIR SHAPES, ADD EYES AND A MOUTH, DRAW ALL THE DETAILS, AND FINISH BY OUTLINING WITH A MARKER AND ERASING THE PENCIL TO COLOR AS YOU LIKE.

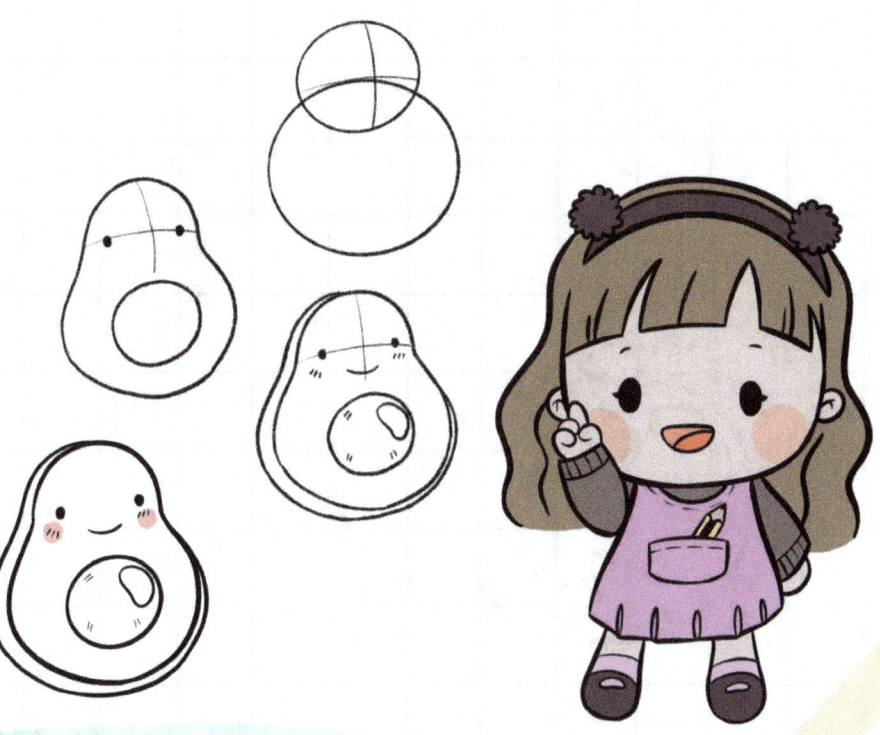

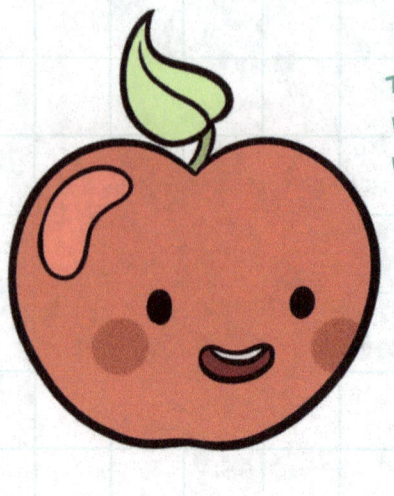

TO DRAW AN APPLE, WE'LL START WITH A CIRCLE. WE'LL CONTINUE WITH THE DETAILS OF ITS SHAPE AND KAWAII EXPRESSION.

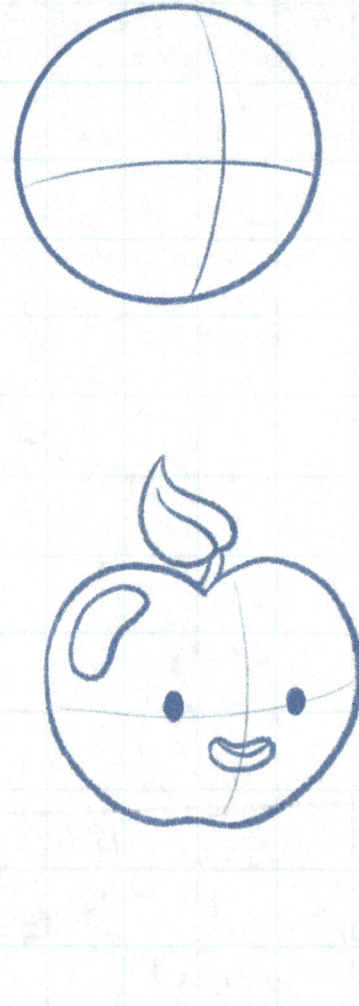

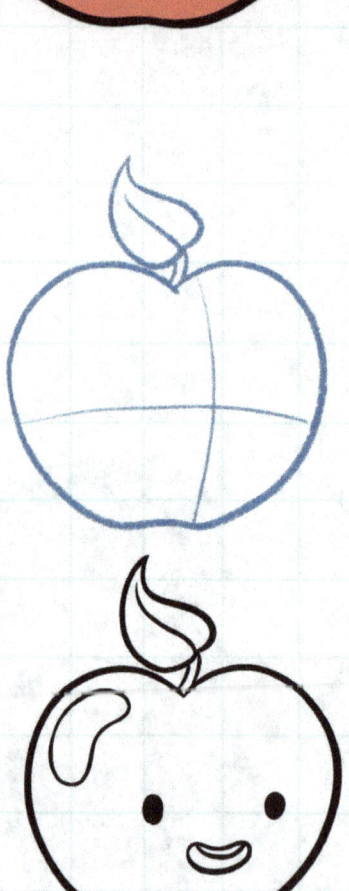

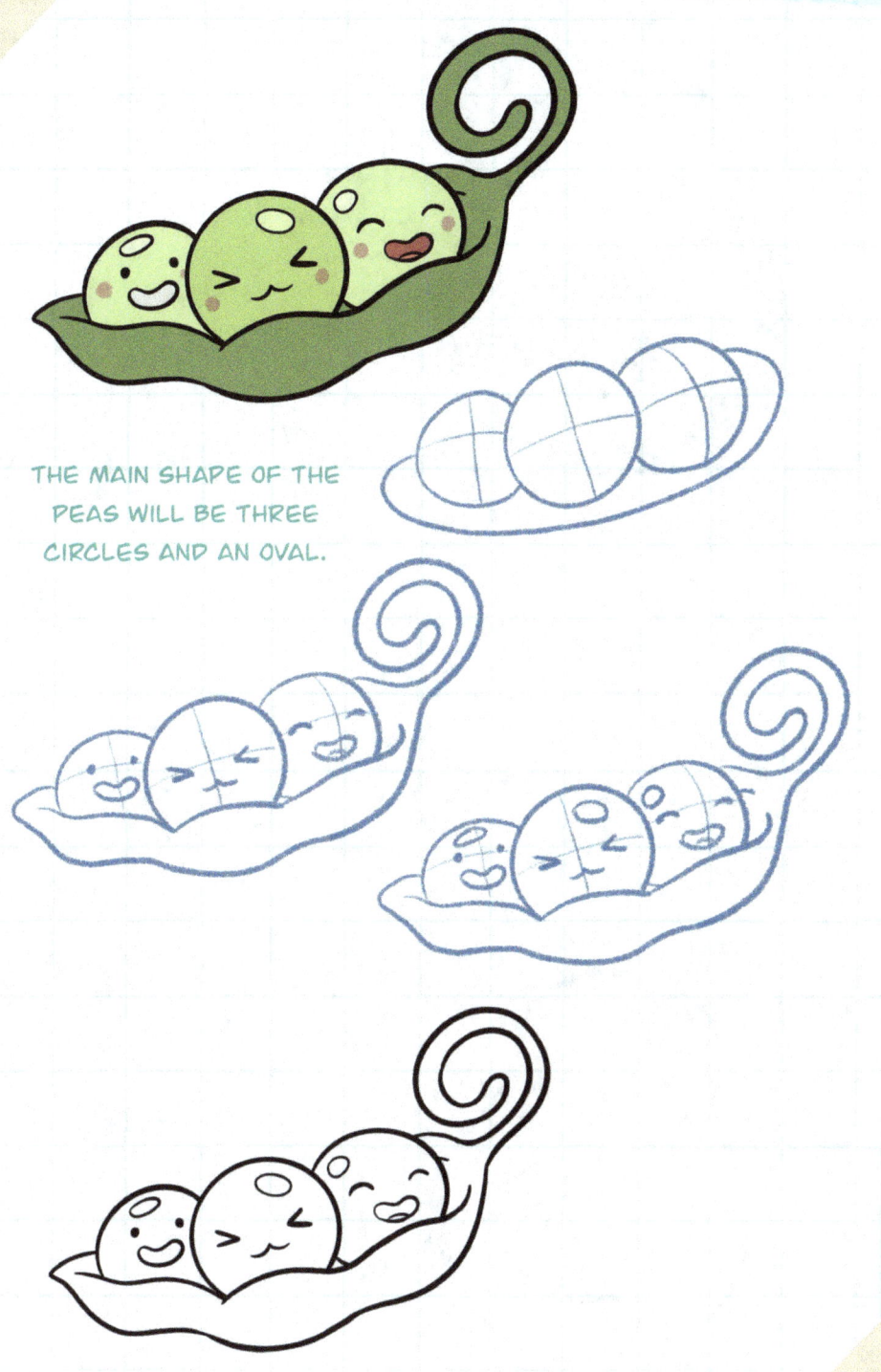

THE MAIN SHAPE OF THE
PEAS WILL BE THREE
CIRCLES AND AN OVAL.

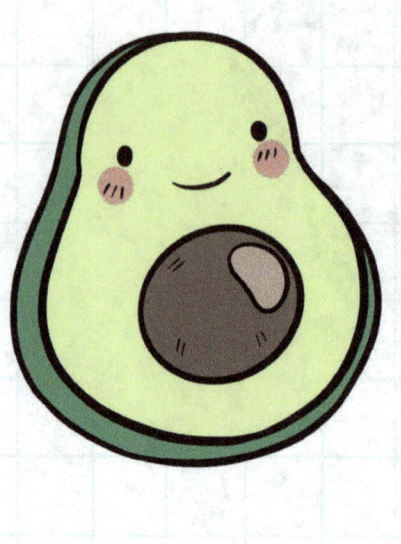

THE AVOCADO STARTS WITH ITS MAIN SHAPE, WHICH IS TWO CIRCLES, AND IN THE NEXT STEP, WE ADD A THIRD CIRCLE IN ITS BELLY, WHICH WILL BE THE PIT.

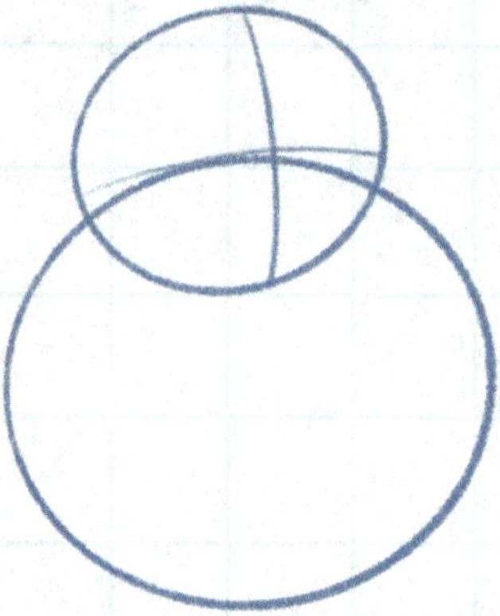

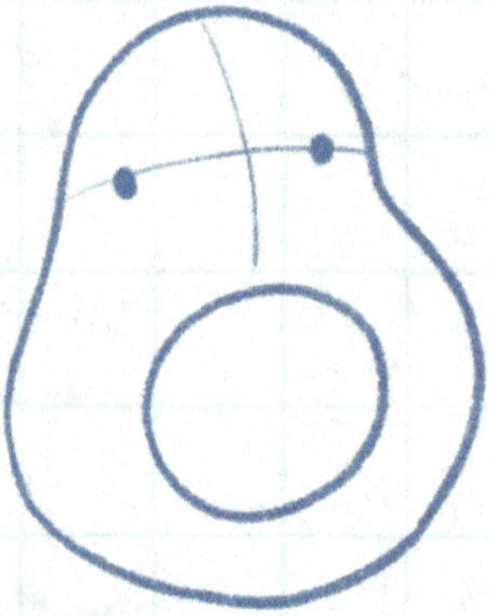

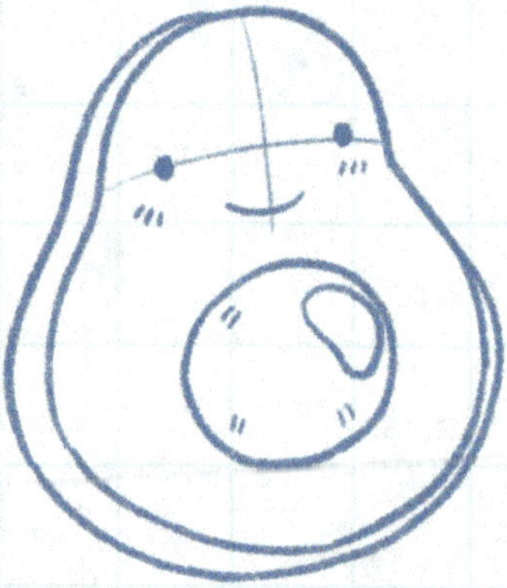

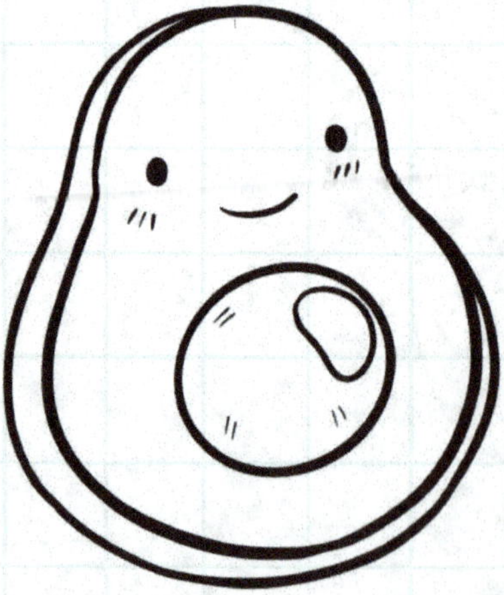

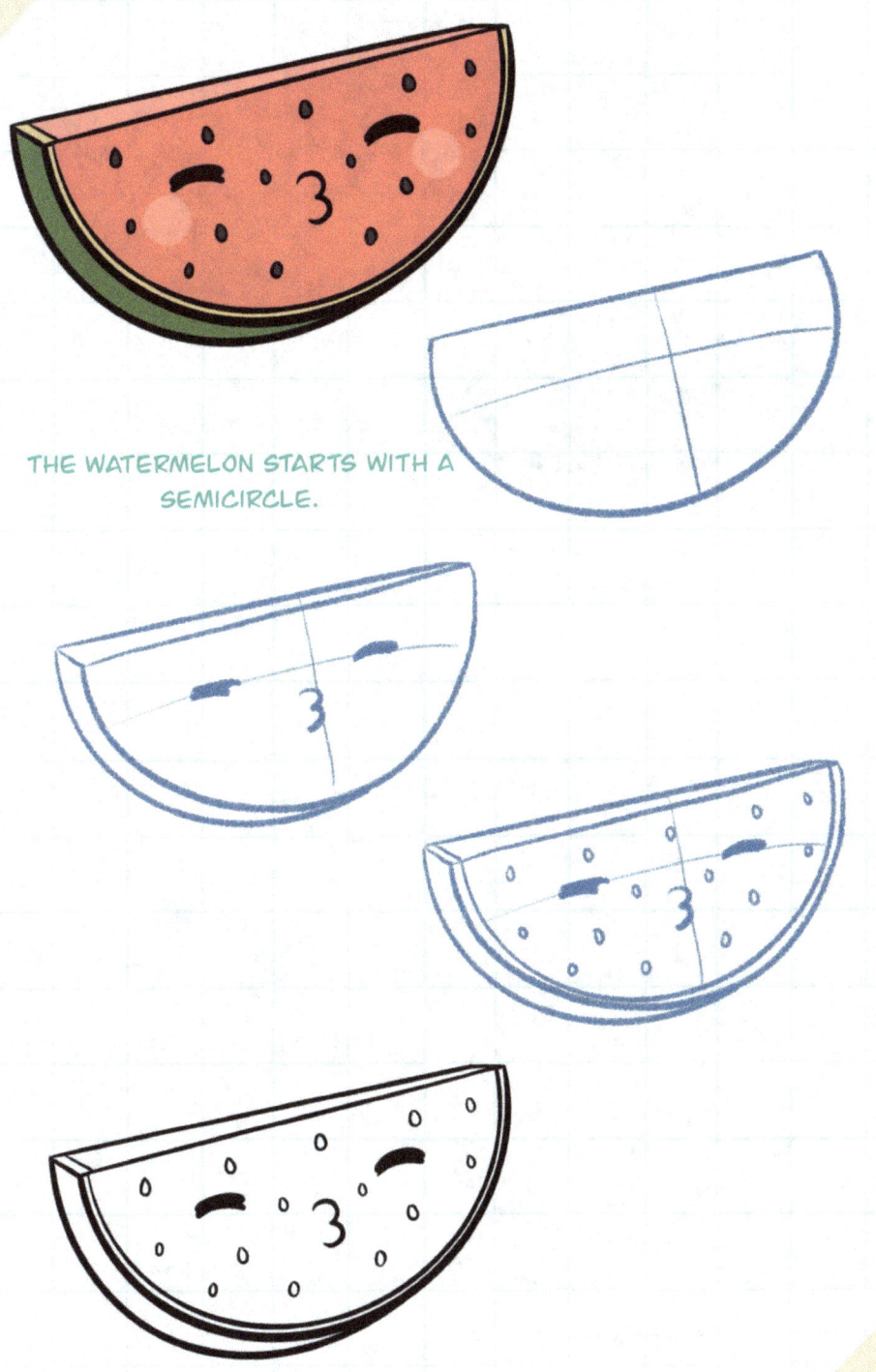

THE WATERMELON STARTS WITH A SEMICIRCLE.

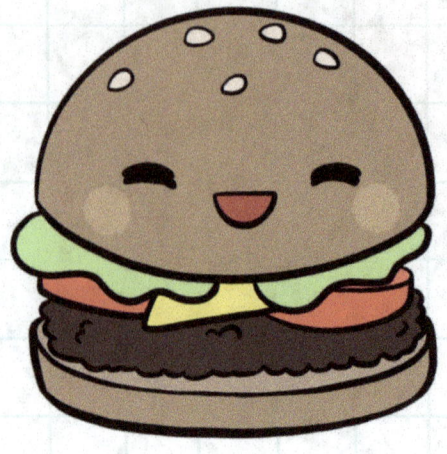

TO START DRAWING THE HAMBURGER, WE'LL MAKE A CIRCLE AND A SQUARE TO GIVE IT HEIGHT.

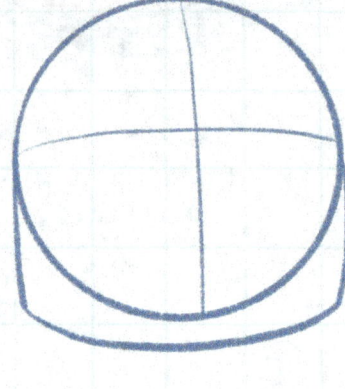

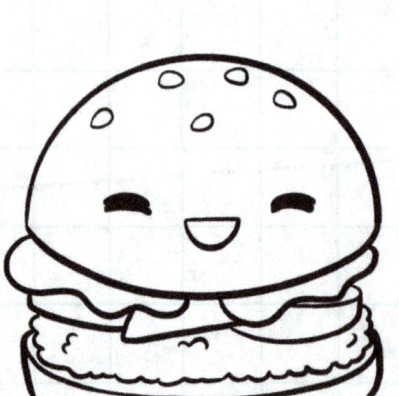

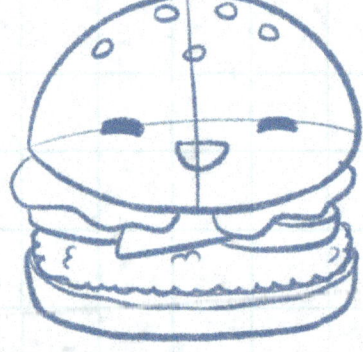

WE'LL PLACE THE KAWAII EXPRESSION ON THE BUN, AND IN THE MIDDLE PART, WE'LL DRAW THE INGREDIENTS.

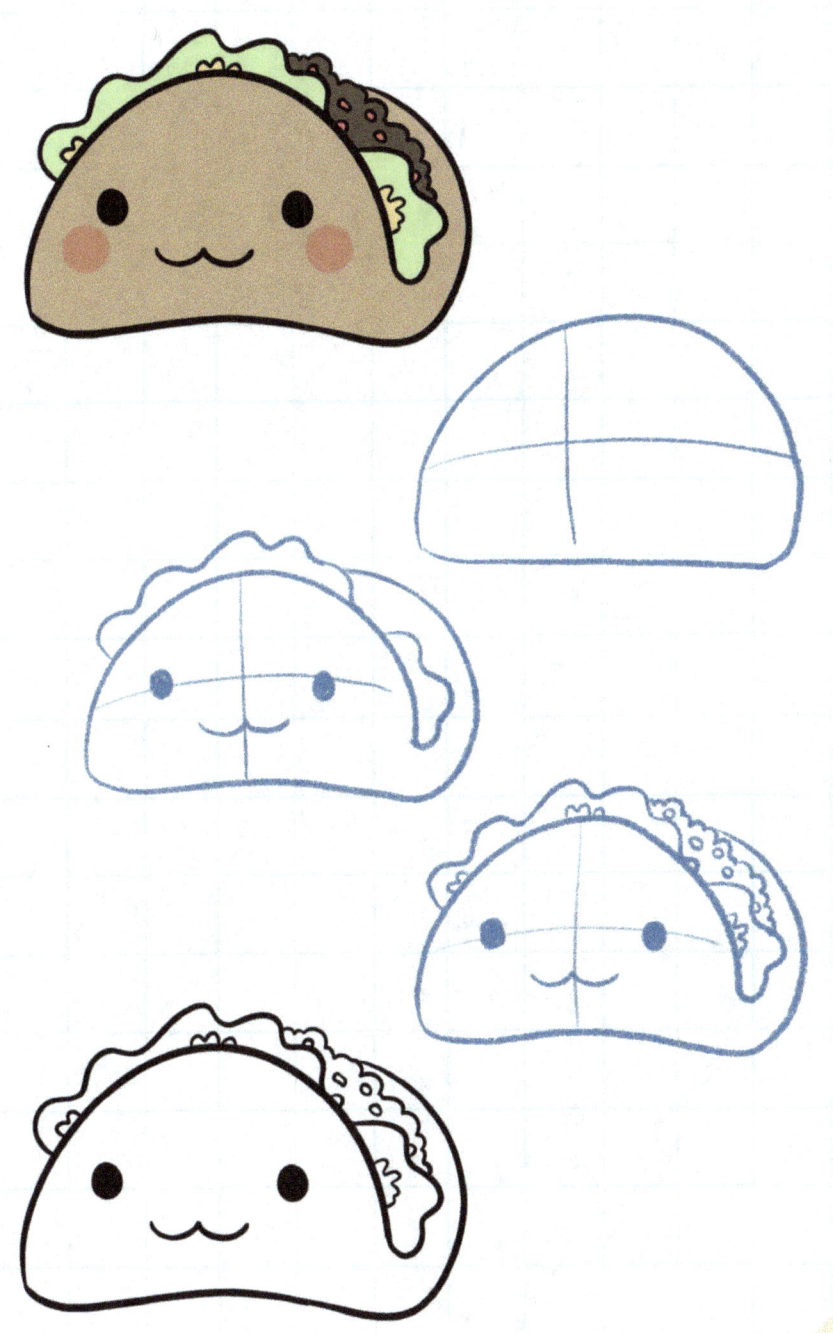

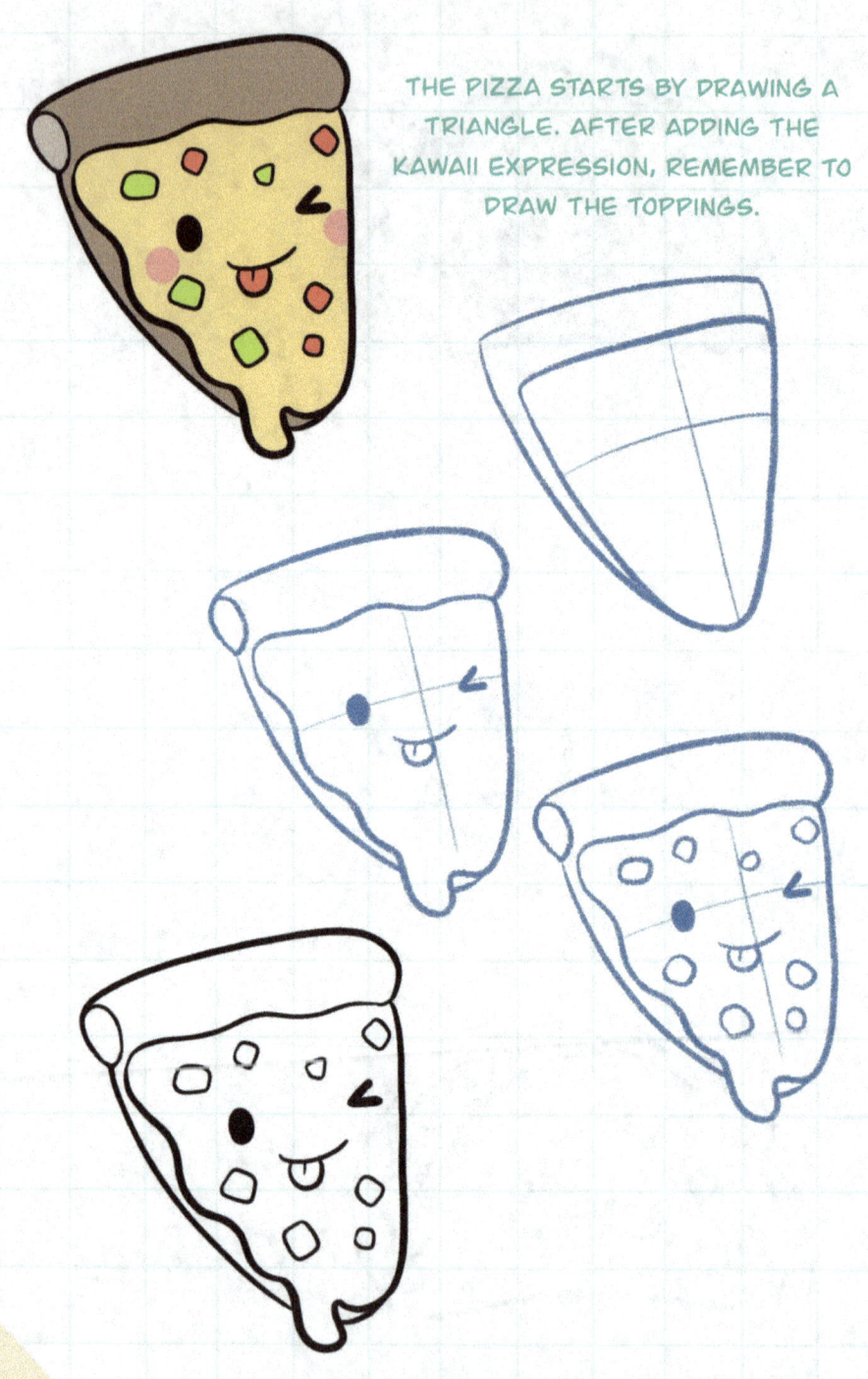

THE PIZZA STARTS BY DRAWING A TRIANGLE. AFTER ADDING THE KAWAII EXPRESSION, REMEMBER TO DRAW THE TOPPINGS.

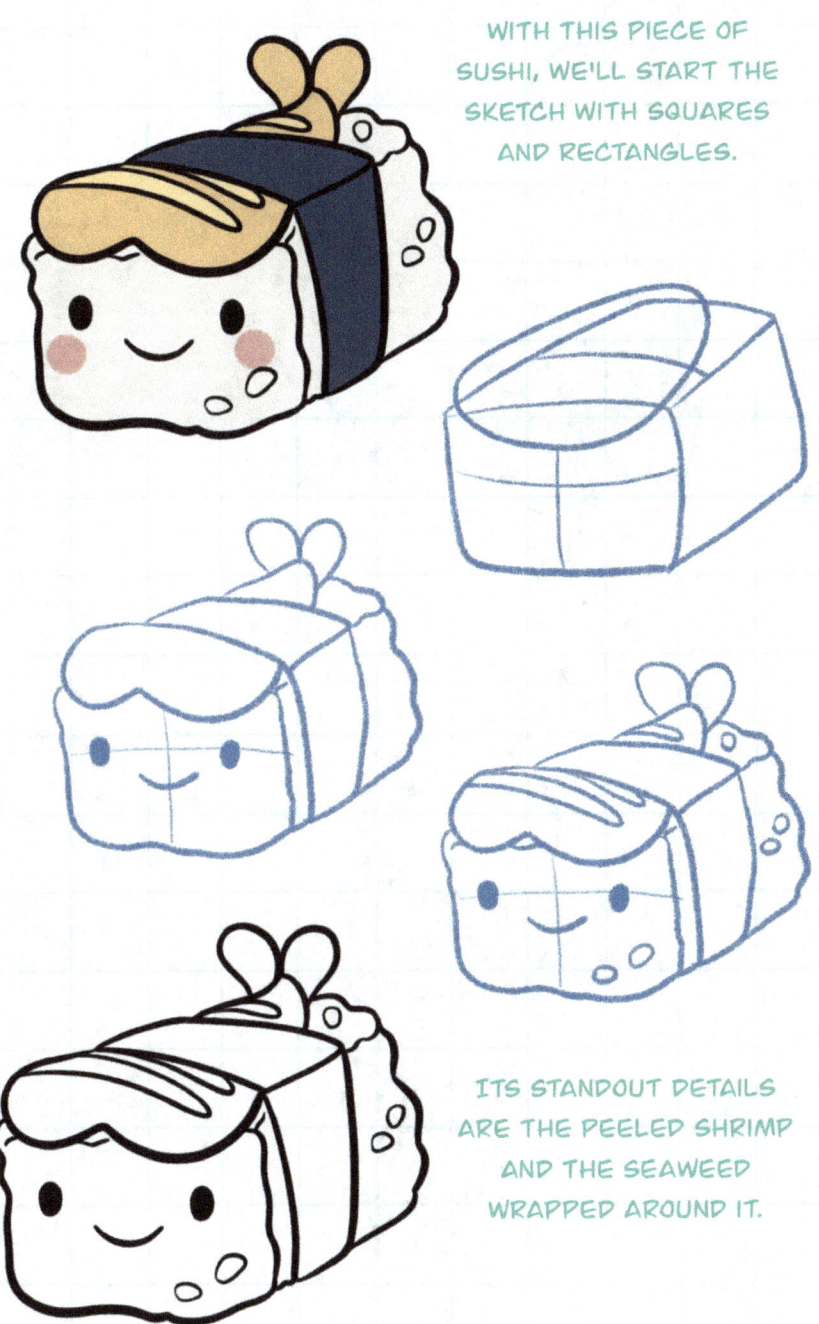

WITH THIS PIECE OF
SUSHI, WE'LL START THE
SKETCH WITH SQUARES
AND RECTANGLES.

ITS STANDOUT DETAILS
ARE THE PEELED SHRIMP
AND THE SEAWEED
WRAPPED AROUND IT.

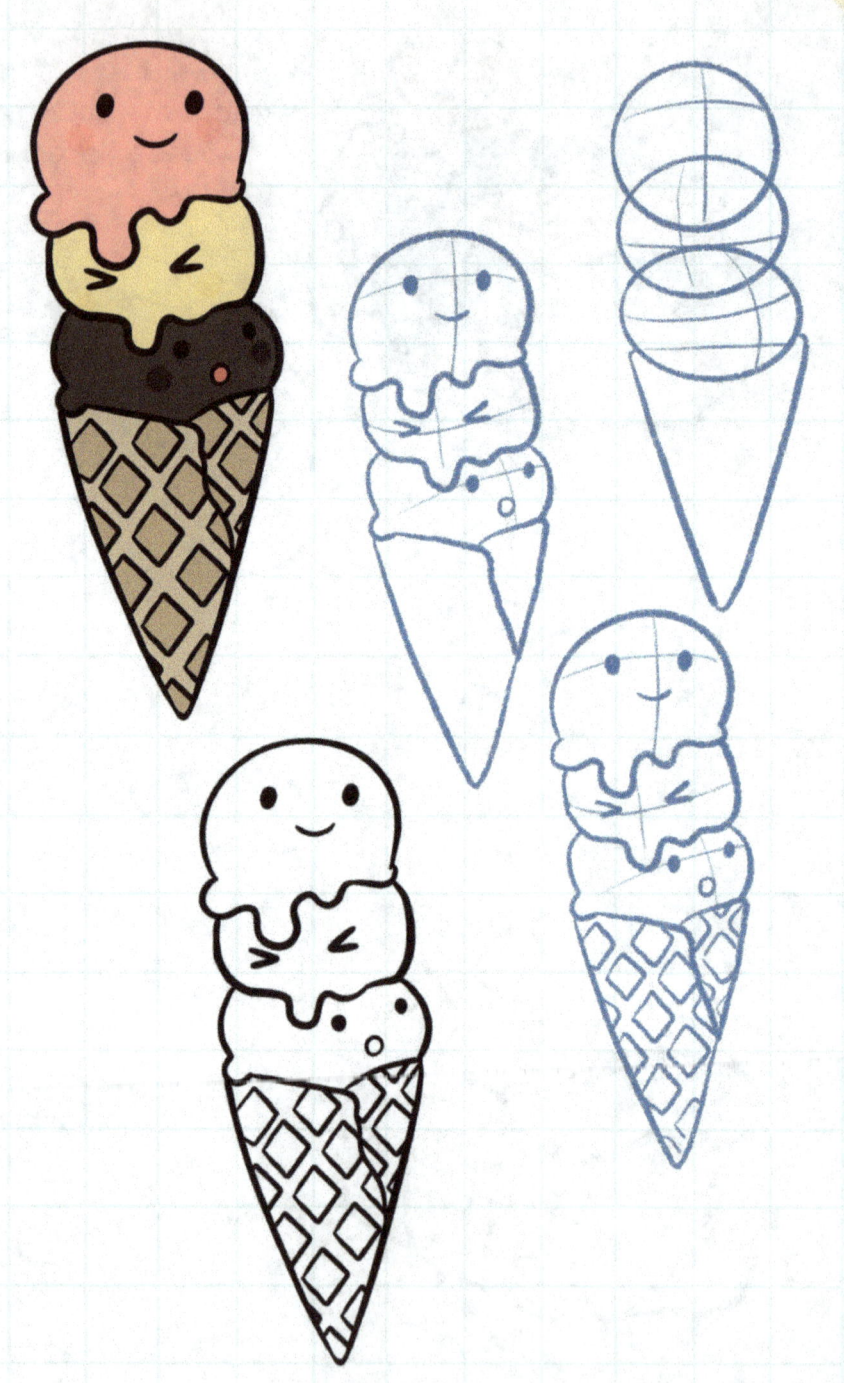

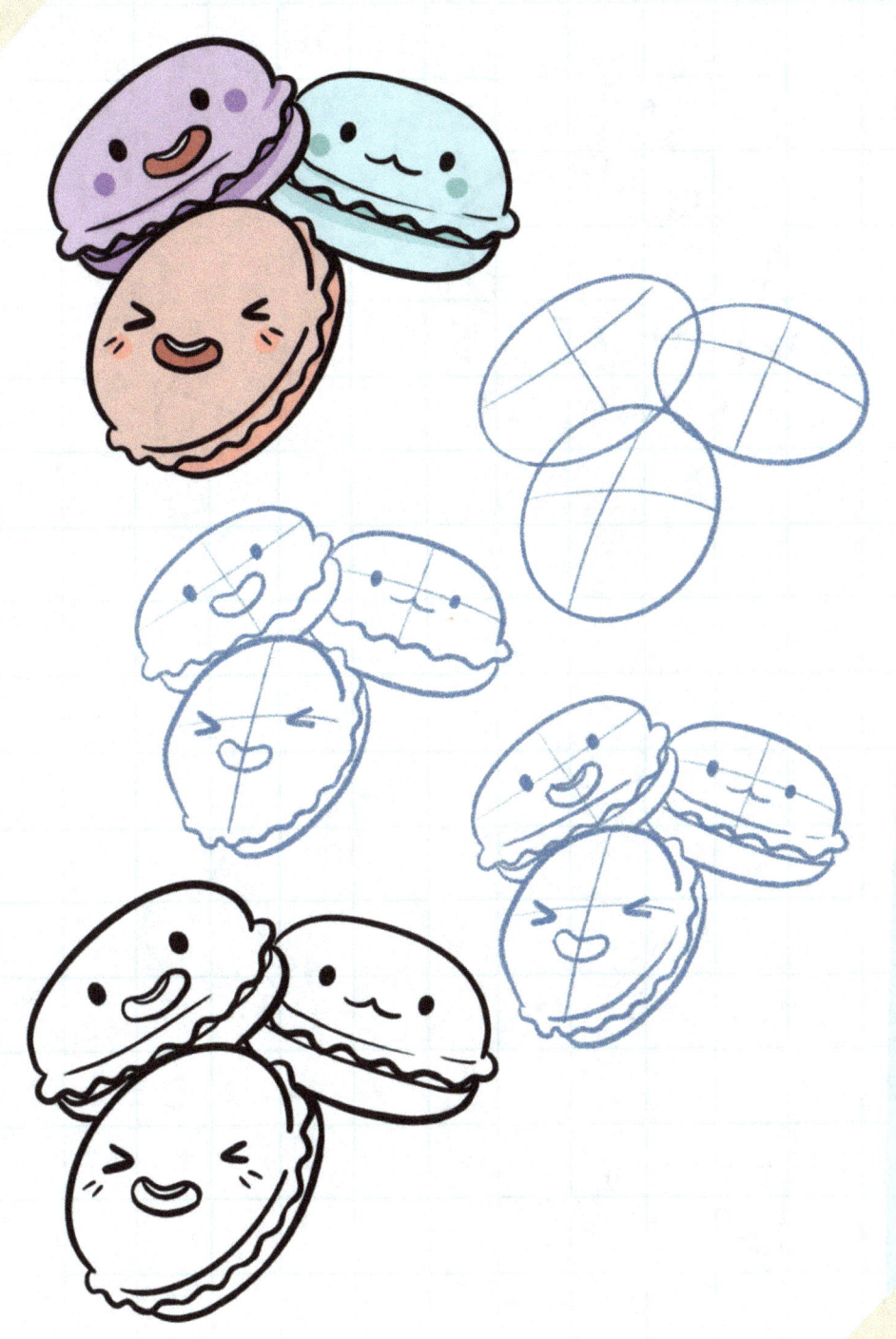

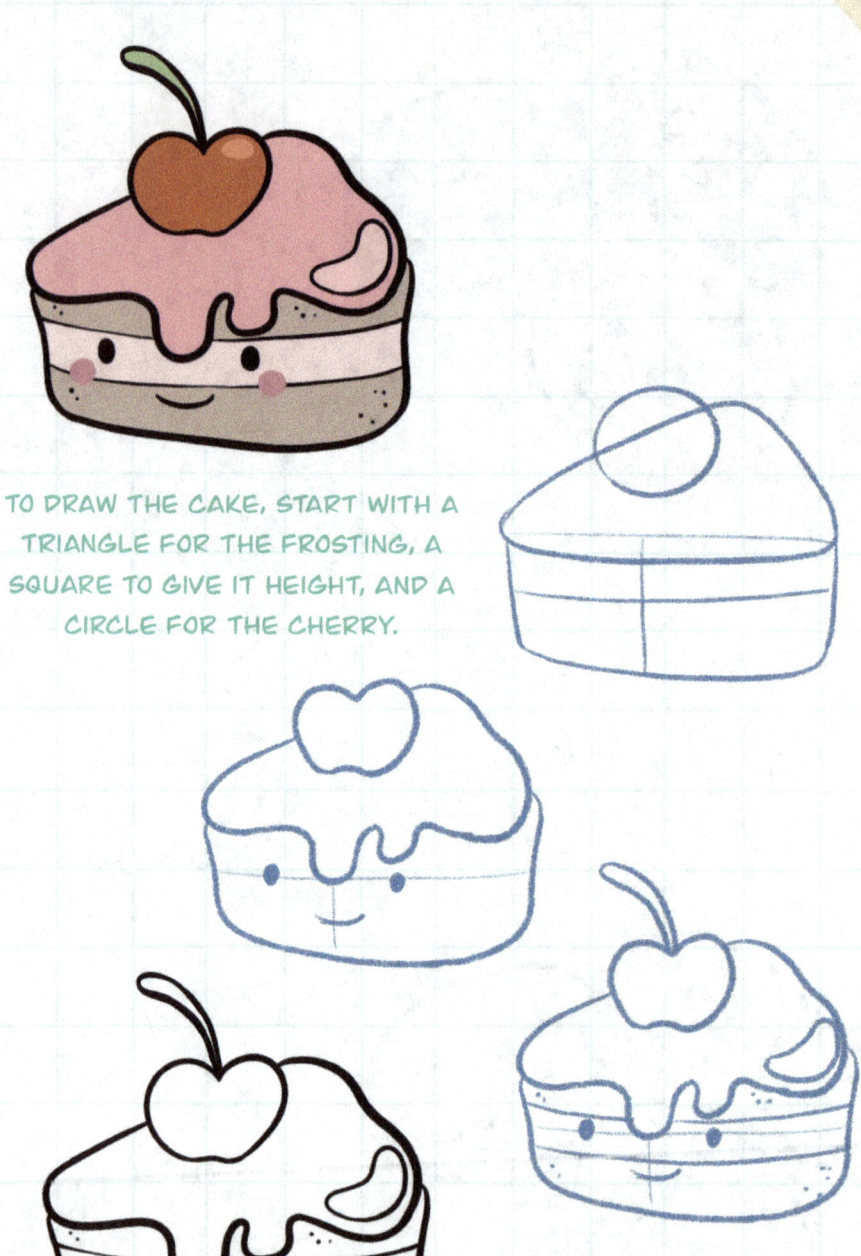

TO DRAW THE CAKE, START WITH A TRIANGLE FOR THE FROSTING, A SQUARE TO GIVE IT HEIGHT, AND A CIRCLE FOR THE CHERRY.

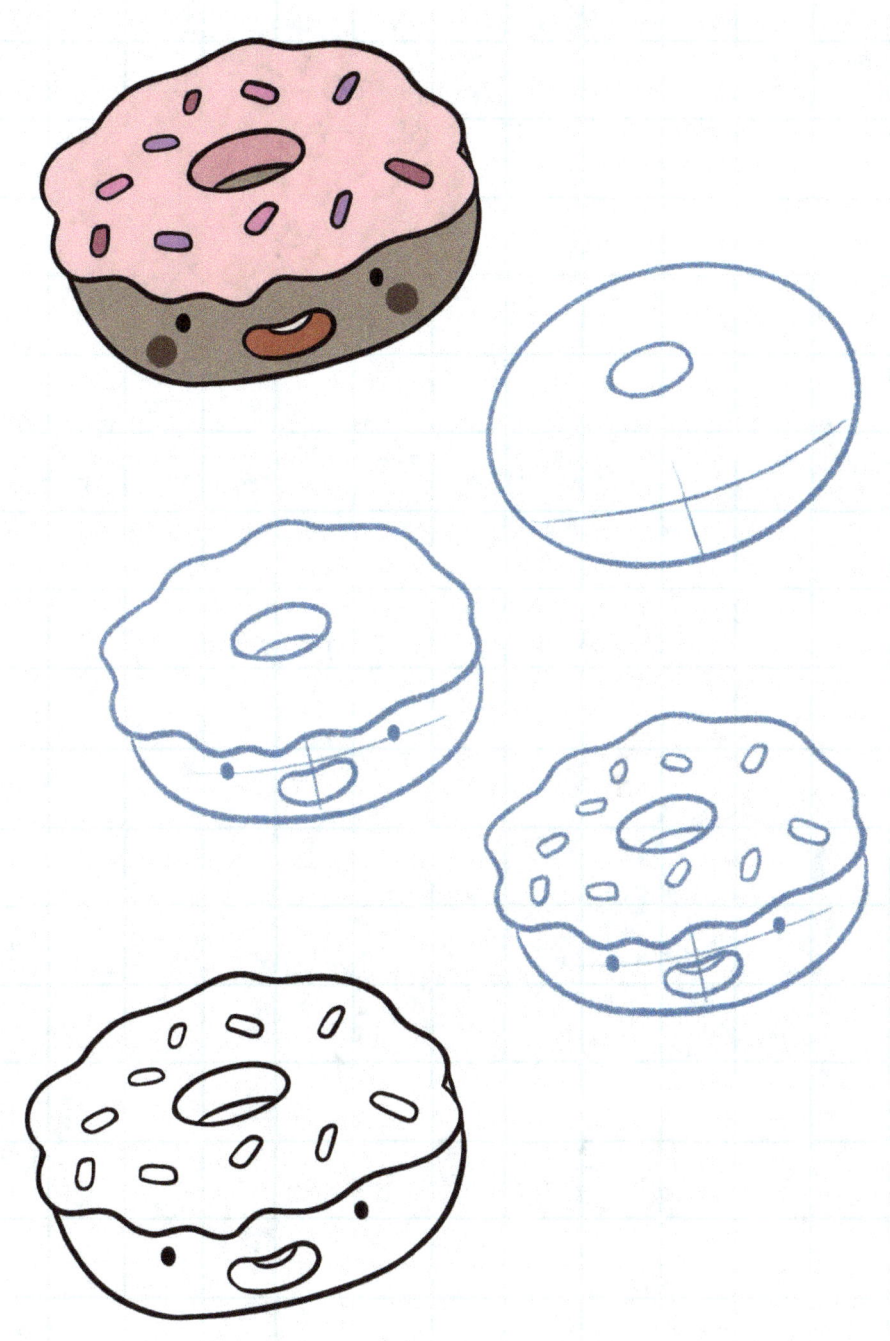

CONTINUING OUR WORK, IT WOULD BE A GREAT HONOR IF YOU COULD REVIEW US WITH YOUR OPINION AND FIVE STARS ON AMAZON.

FROM SAORI BOOKS, WE HAVE MORE BOOKS THAT WE KNOW YOU'LL LOVE. YOU CAN FIND THEM ON AMAZON.

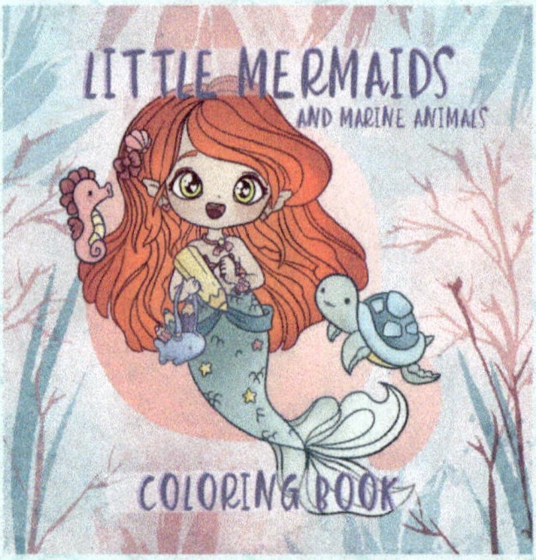

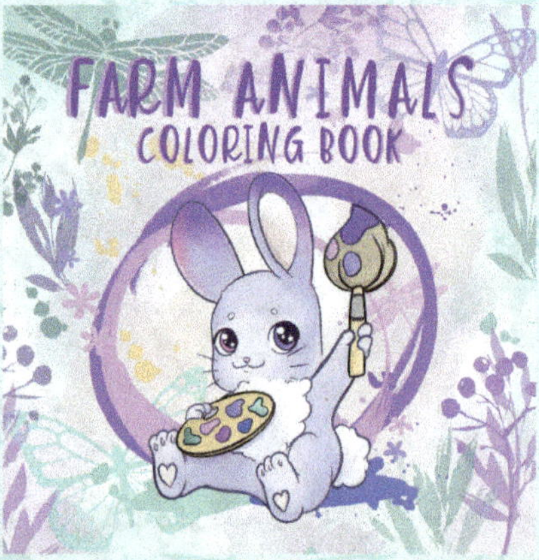

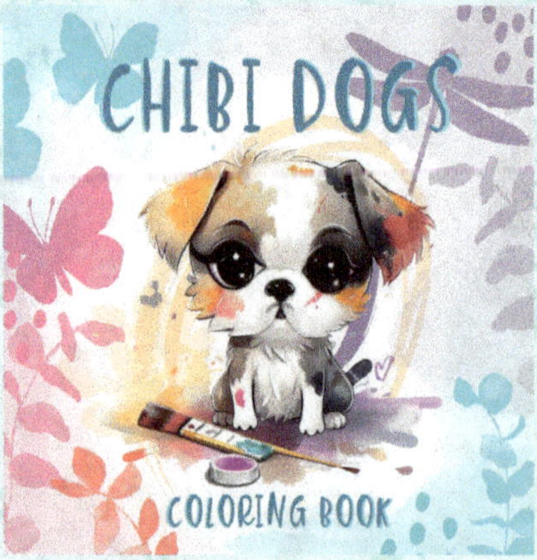

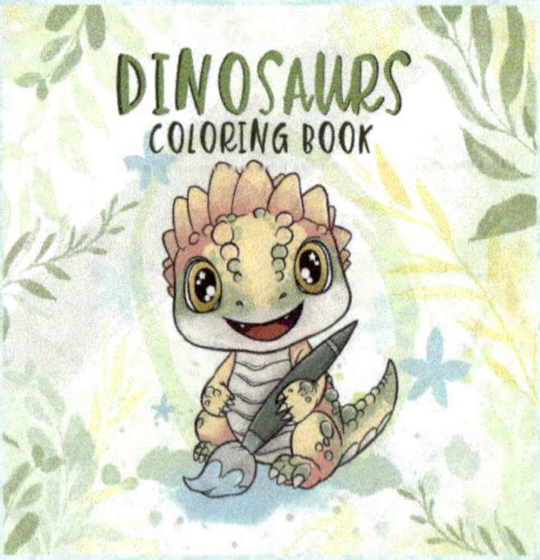